Longhorns for Life

By
Whit Canning

SportsPublishingLLC.com

ISBN 10: 1-59670-123-4
ISBN 13: 978-1-59670-123-6

Publishers: Peter L. Bannon and Joseph J. Bannon Sr.
Senior managing editor: Susan M. Moyer
Acquisitions editor: Mike Pearson
Developmental editor: Aaron Geiger
Art director: K. Jeffrey Higgerson
Dust jacket design: Dustin Hubbart
Interior layout: Heidi Norsen
Photo editor: Erin Linden-Levy

Sports Publishing L.L.C.
804 North Neil Street
Champaign, IL 61820
Phone: 1-877-424-2665
Fax: 217-363-2073
SportsPublishingLLC.com

Printed in the United States of America

Library of Congress Cataloging-in-Publication Data

Canning, Whit.
    Longhorns for life / by Whit Canning.
    p. cm.
    ISBN-13: 978-1-59670-123-6 (alk. paper)
    ISBN-10: 1-59670-123-4 (alk. paper)
    1. University of Texas at Austin--Football--History. 2. Texas Longhorns (Football team)--History. I. Title.
    GV956.T47C36 2006
    796.332'630976431--dc22
                                    2006021961

Contents

Acknowledgments

I would like to extend my sincere gratitude to the many individuals who graciously lent their time and expertise to the completion of this project. Included among these are the more than 25 men and women who shared their feelings and experiences in the interviews that make up the character and color of this project. In many instances, they also became valuable sources pointing me toward new subjects that became valuable additions to the book.

And thanks also to Sheila Eveslage, Bill Little, and Maria Spitler from the University of Texas; Trey McLean, Texas Exes; Kirk Bohls, *Austin American-Statesman*; Bo Carter, Big 12 Conference; and the staff at Sports Publishing.

Sources:
The Alcalde
Austin American-Statesman
Backyard Brawl by W. K. Stratton, Three Rivers Press, 2003
The Cowboys
Dallas Morning News
Fort Worth Star-Telegram
Here Come the Texas Longhorns by Lou Maysel
Los Angeles Times
Southwest Conference Baseball's Greatest Hits by Neal Farmer,
    Eakin Press, 1996
Stadium Stories: Texas Longhorns by Bill Little,
    The Globe Pequot Press, 2005
Texas Football Media Guide
We Are the Aggies by John Adams

1

HARLEY CLARK

Hook 'Em Horns

At age 70, Harley Clark has a confession to make. "Tomatoes seem to like me," he says.

OK. Well there are worse things that could happen ...

Clark, a retired senior district judge now living the good life with his wife, Patti, was actually referring to his skill at growing tomatoes, which is part of what the couple is into these days. "I hung it up in '99," he says, "and moved to Dripping Springs, property we've owned for 30 years, built a house on. Now I grow organic vegetables and sell them to fancy restaurants in Austin."

The tomatoes, in particular, are a great success. "We really get along well," he says. "I've got a little greenhouse, and I start all my plants from seeds myself. Last year we sold 2,957 pounds of tomatoes ... and hell, I don't know how many I gave away and ate, probably another 500 pounds. That's a little over 30 pounds per bush. I had about 95 vines. It's incredible."

If this continues, Clark may one day be universally renowned for his tomatoes. Then again, it's unlikely. As far as universally renowned goes, he's already got that covered.

In fact, on November 11, 2005, they threw a big party in Gregory Gym, the very spot where—50 years before—Clark achieved Texas immortality.

On November 11, 1955, Clark—then UT's head cheerleader—addressed a pep rally before a big game and offered the faithful a little something extra: an odd-looking hand signal that he said they should flash at the game the next day to show their support.

The gesture was destined to become—forever—the sign of the Longhorns: Hook 'em Horns.

Over five decades, legions of Longhorn fans have flashed that sign millions of times as an emblem of their allegiance, to the point that by Texas standards, it has become as ubiquitous as Coke. The day that he introduced it, Clark stood on the stage and watched as students tried to form the sign with their fingers and learn how to do it. For UT fans now, it is as automatic as if they came out of the crib flashing it.

On all occasions—whether joyous, symbolic, reverent, or menacing—Texas fans raise their horns for solidarity and comfort. Along with the Longhorn emblem itself, the Hook 'em sign has become the identifying trademark of the school's athletic teams. It has even achieved fame in the strongholds of the school's most bitter rivals. Among Sooners and Aggies, flashing the sign upside down with the horns pointing downward, is thought to be the most effective way to insult a Longhorn.

The actual inventor was Henry Pitts, one of Clark's fellow students. It was an idea born of desperation and did not exactly produce overwhelming success in its debut. But it caught on instantly with UT students and quickly became the essential symbol of UT spirit and pride.

In 1955, Clark was a junior at UT, and in his second year on the cheerleading squad. The Longhorns were also in their second year—of mediocrity—as the tenure of Ed Price began to unravel. A popular former player and assistant coach, Price became the head coach at the wrong time and was destined to become an unfortunate footnote: the man who preceded Darrell Royal.

The once-dominant program had slipped badly the previous year, and the '55 team opened the season by losing four of its first five games.

In that span, the Longhorns were soundly beaten by national powers Southern Cal and Oklahoma, and even lost to Texas Tech, which was not yet a member of the Southwest Conference. They also lost the SWC opener to Arkansas, the defending champion.

They suddenly recovered with a three-game winning streak against Rice, SMU, and Baylor, evening the season record at 4-4. More importantly, they were 3-1 in conference play and had a chance to possibly win the championship and go to the Cotton Bowl. But the last two wins had each been by one point, and those close to the program realized it was probably living on borrowed time. On November 12, the Longhorns were scheduled to host TCU.

Led by All-America halfback Jim Swink, the Horned Frogs were the most powerful team in the conference, with an upset three-point loss to the Aggies their only blemish.

"That year," Clark says, "I had been elected head cheerleader by the student body. That was back in the days when the student body elected everybody. Then the head cheerleader conducted a contest to elect seven or eight others. So I figured I had an elected office there, you see, and I figured that office was slightly more important than the governorship.

"Things were a little different back then. Cheerleaders today are sort of like circus acrobats. We did cheers then sort of like the Aggies do now—there wasn't all of that flipping pretty girls up in the air. But also, back in those days the head cheerleader was also the captain of the field. Part of my job was deciding when the yells would be, what the yells would be, when the band would play, and what would be going on down on the field. I don't know who does all that now, but it's changed a lot. They may not even still have a head cheerleader."

And so, in times of crisis there were decisions to be made, and Clark was not a man to shirk his responsibilities. "It was obvious that we had a mediocre team," he says. "But we had a chance to win at least a part of the Southwest Conference title if we could beat TCU. They had a great team, and Jim Swink was a wonderful player.

"So the spirit was building up to beat TCU, and we were trying to make up in spirit what we lacked in football talent. So we planned a big pep rally for Gregory Gym. There was also a variety show planned by the Campus Chest in conjunction with the pep rally, and we were looking for any kind of extra boost we could find."

Enter Henry Pitts: stout fellow, loyal friend, and inventive genius.

"About Monday or Tuesday," Clark says, "Henry came up to me and showed me how if you did your hand a certain way, you could make it look like the head of a Longhorn. So I carried that idea around for a couple of days—tried it out on a few people, fellow students, friends. They weren't real impressed. One of them said it was too corny and another— my best friend—said, 'Naw, that'll never do.'

"But I thought it was a natural. And at that time, the only other college or university I knew of that had a hand sign was the Aggies. There wasn't any other school anywhere that had a hand sign, other than A&M. This sign looked like a perfect natural for us. So I decided that at the end of the rally, as a special effort, so to speak, to raise spirit, I would get everybody quiet, show them how to do this, and proclaim it as our official hand sign.

"So we had the variety show and the pep rally, and Gregory Gym was full—there must have been four or five thousand people there—and I got everybody quiet, and I told them.

"I had mine already made, and I held it up and I said, 'If you do your hands like this, it'll look like the head of a Longhorn. Y'all go ahead and try it.' I could see 'em all down there kind of fumbling around with it, trying to get used to it.

I could see some of them moving their fingers around with their other hand, trying to get it to work. And I mentioned the Aggies' sign and I said it was time for us to have one of our own.

"I said, 'Hold 'em up,' and everybody held their horns up, and I officially proclaimed it the new hand sign of the University of Texas—'to be used wherever and whenever Longhorns gather. So use it tomorrow at the game and after that use it forever.' So we did one short yell and used the Hook 'em Horns sign, and the rally was over.

"Standing up there on the stage, I was watching them walk out, cutting up, goring each other, having fun with it … and you could tell, right then, it was gonna stick. You knew it was going to work."

This was not, however, a unanimous viewpoint.

"We had a dean back then named Arno Nowotny," Clark says, "and he walked up behind me on the stage—I didn't know he was there—and grabbed me by the elbow and wheeled me around. He was a little short guy, and I looked down at him and I could tell he was mad, and he said, 'Harley, I am furious with you!'

"And I said, 'Dean, what's the matter with you?' and he said, 'Look at that sign out there! This is going to stick—it will become our official hand sign! You have not run this by me to get my permission to make this our official sign, and I have not taken this up to the president of the university to get permission for *you* to proclaim this our hand sign.

"I said, 'Dean, everybody really likes this.' He kind of fell silent for a minute. Then he made a Hook 'em Horns sign and stuck it up in my face and said, 'Harley, do you know what this means in Sicily?'"

Well, no, Clark did not know what it meant in Sicily, but it has since become reasonably clear. Longhorns traveling in Italy and Sicily are always warned not to put the horns up, because it is considered an obscene gesture. Something to do with a slur upon one's mother. Clark's actual response, as he recalls, was, "Dean, I don't know anything. I'm 19."

At the game the next day, the new Hook 'em sign was an immediate success. The Longhorns weren't. "Just looking around before the game," Clark says, "you could see the students practicing it and fooling around with it, and we used it throughout the game, and you could sort of see it creep around the stadium. It went around the horseshoe and over onto the non-student side, and by the end of the first half everybody in the stadium was doing it."

The sign was to little avail—Swink had the greatest game of his glittering career, rushing for 235 yards and four touchdowns, and the Horns were buried, 47–20. This, despite the fact that Texas also rolled out the "Red Candle Hex"—normally reserved for the Aggies—to cast an additional spell on the Frogs.

"We were burning the red candles like crazy that week," Clark says. "All over Austin, there were hundreds of red candles. Some of them real, some of them mocked up … some people made great big ones that were not real but looked like it, and they'd put a light bulb in them and burn it all night long.

"What prompted it was that Willie Morris was the editor of the *Daily Texan* then, and he wrote a front-page editorial going through the history of the red candles and urging people to do it. But I guess we put a little tarnish on that tradition."

The new hand sign tradition was redeemed 12 days later when the Longhorns pulled a stunning 21–6 upset of Texas A&M, knocking the Aggies out of contention for the championship, which was won by TCU. At the end of the A&M game, the Hook 'em sign was firmly established as a new tradition at UT, and Clark's cheerleading career was over. In his senior year, he was elected student body president.

"Got into politics," he says.

In 1957, Royal became the head coach, and the Longhorns began winning again, and the new tradition steadily gained strength. Clark went on to a long and successful career that included 13 years on the bench.

"I still get a kick of it," he says, "when I'm at some really serious, dignified event … you'll maybe see the president of the university up there at commencement, dressed in all his academic regalia, flashing the Hook 'em sign."

Reminded that it has long been possible to go into the campus bookstore at OU and buy a T-shirt with an inverted Hook 'em Horns sign, Clark laughs. "I love it," he says.

It was all worth a festive anniversary celebration last fall, when Gregory Gym was filled once again and nearly 2,000 cardboard hands in the shape of the famous sign were distributed.

The Texas Exes Heritage Society arranged the event, and the crowd included many alumni who had attended the original rally 50 years earlier, displaying a banner that read, "We were here then, and we're here now!"

Gordon Wynne, who along with Bob Armstrong (who later became the Texas Land Commissioner) produced the original variety show, wrote an original anniversary song. U.S. Senator Kay Bailey Hutchison, a former UT cheerleader, was one of the speakers.

UT president Larry Faulkner authorized the Texas Tower to be lit up orange, with a "50" in the windows. During the several days of the event, Clark and Pitts spent much of their time autographing Hook 'em T-shirts. "It was amazing," Clark says. "I must have signed two or three thousand T-shirts."

The fanfare done, Clark returned to the life of gentleman farmer in Dripping Springs. "We've got three large areas fenced off and irrigated," he says, "and we grow different things seasonally. Our produce has become very popular with some of the restaurants in Austin, and that's basically what we do now the year 'round.

"No more working inside for ol' Harley."

2

War Hero Returns to Texas

In October of 1945, Sergeant Frank Denius was riding an Army troop train following a meandering course south from the East Coast toward the Red River, carrying a cargo of discharged veterans.

"Back then," he says, "those trains were just a string of boxcars with hammocks in them for you to sleep in. There was no dining car ... they had to stop and let you off to eat. For that matter, they had to stop and let you off to use the bathroom.

"When we got to St. Louis, I went up and asked the engineer what time we would arrive in Texarkana, and he said sometime between five and six the next morning.

I made sure I was awake. When we arrived, I got off at the station and looked around and found a flagpole. I walked over and saluted the flag. Then I got down on my hands and knees and kissed the ground. I was finally back home ... in Texas."

He was not yet old enough to vote or legally buy a drink. But he wore four Silver Stars and two Purple Hearts—one of the most decorated soldiers returning from World War II.

"I guess it seemed to me like the world was moving pretty fast back then," he says, smiling. "I used to tell people that when we landed in Europe I was 18 years old, and when we left I was 40. And it sometimes still seems amazing that in '45, I was still over there fighting the Germans on May 7, and by October 30 I was sitting in a class at the University of Texas. It was something that I had thought about for a long time. I decided when I was young that I wanted to go to law school, and I always wanted to go to the university. And so, that's where I was."

It was also at about that point that the Longhorns played a home football game, which Denius attended. He hasn't missed one since. In fact, over the entire span of 60 years, Denius has missed a total of seven games—all on the road, all due to severe weather. The last time it happened was Christmas Day 1982, when Texas was playing in the Sun Bowl.

"We took a charter flight out there in the morning," he says, "but when we got to El Paso, we ran into a big snowstorm. We circled the airport for an hour and a half, and then it got worse. Finally, the pilot came on and said we couldn't land and we would have to return to Austin. That's the last game I've missed."

He does admit, though, to missing three *practices* this year, as if owning up to some deep personal failure. In the years since he rode that troop train back from the war, Denius—who has practiced law in Austin since getting his degree in 1949 and has had his own practice for 30 years—has become strongly identified with the University.

He and Charmaine, his wife of 56 years, have raised two children—both UT grads—and steadfastly supported the university in every way possible.

The football team's practice facility is named after him. The concourse of the alumni center is named after him. The Normandy Scholar Program—which dispatches an annual pilgrimage of Texas students to the famous battlefield for tours and studies—is named after him.

This year, Denius received a Presidential Citation in recognition of a lifetime of support for his alma mater, with a letter citing his "renowned service" and "profound contributions" in helping the university achieve its mission. Over the years, countless UT grads have counted on him as friend, advisor, and benefactor.

He plays chess with Darrell Royal.

"The university is part of my family's life," he says. "It's just been such a great experience for all of us, myself, my wife, my children, to be associated with UT."

His story began 81 years ago in Athens, where Denius says he was "raised mostly by my mother and grandmother—my parents divorced when I was eight years old.

"By the time I was 12 it was apparent that a war was coming on, and it was felt that I would be best prepared by going to a military school, so I went to Schreiner Institute over in Kerrville, which at that time consisted of four years of high school and then junior college. I finished high school in three and a half years and did one semester of college. Then when I turned 17, I joined the Army. They had a program back then where if you signed up at 17 they would send you to college for a couple of semesters before you were called to active duty. So I spent a year at The Citadel in 1942-43, and then in late spring I took a three-week course at UT in freshman English. I was called to active duty on June 1, 1943."

Denius went through basic training and an artillery course and then boarded a troop ship early in 1944. "When we got to England, we went through Ranger training," he says. "Then I was assigned to the 30th Infantry Division, and we began preparing for the invasion."

It was a fateful posting. By the end of the war, the 30th infantry was one of the most renowned combat divisions in the American army, and for Denius, life was indeed moving swiftly.

When he landed on the Normandy beachhead in June of '44, he was a private. By the time his unit reached the Elbe River late in the spring of '45, he was a battle-hardened sergeant.

"I was with the 230th Field Artillery Battalion of the 30th infantry," he says. "The 29th division's artillery was lost at Omaha Beach, and we were rushed in to support them. There were two divisions there—the 1st Infantry, which was a regular army division, and the 29th, which was a National Guard division from Virginia and that area. Their 115th Artillery Regiment suffered 80 percent casualties and was wiped out, so for the first six days we gave them artillery support. Then we moved back to our division."

Recalling the impact on an 18-year-old kid from East Texas, Denius says, "Without making some kind of dramatic statement about it ... I had known since I was 17 that I was going to have to do this, and we were well-trained and well-prepared. When people say that they weren't scared ... I think you were always scared, but you had to control it because you had a job to do. A lot depended on you carrying out your responsibilities."

Over the next year, none had reason to fault Denius in that regard.

"I was a forward artillery observer," he says. "From there to the end of the war, we took part in every one of the five major battles on that front."

Denius' first Silver Star citation came as a result of a battle on July 17, as the unit was moving inland from Normandy. When the officer directing the artillery fire was killed, private Denius stepped into the breach and directed fire, knocking out tanks and infantry that had held up the American advance.

Then, at Mortagne, France, in early August, the 30th fought its greatest battle. "We were holding a crucial sector, and we were surrounded by 70,000 Germans," Denius says. "And an order came down from General Eisenhower that we were to hold at all costs.

"Basically, it was an 'Alamo' position."

With Denius once again directing the artillery fire, the 30th held for six days, until the German offensive was broken. "It looked pretty bad at the beginning," he says. "But we refused to surrender. We held our ground. It wasn't publicized like Bastogne, but it was one of those battles we absolutely could not afford to lose. If we had not held that position, the Germans would have broken through and cut off Patton's Third Army, and the result could have been disastrous."

Denius also recalls that the battle produced an innovative ploy by one of his commanders that proved most helpful.

"Our supply lines had been cut," he said, "and at one point I radioed back to my battalion commander that we were taking heavy casualties and were badly in need of morphine and penicillin. They had been trying to airlift supplies to us, but we were on a plateau, and the winds would blow the stuff out into an area where if we tried to go out and get it, we came under heavy artillery fire from the Germans.

"So my commander told me he was going to try something different. We had all these propaganda shells that we were always firing at the German positions. There were leaflets inside urging them to surrender, promising that they would be well treated. So my commander took the leaflets out and filled the shells with the morphine and penicillin, wrapped in gauze, and fired them at our position. I directed fire for him and the shells came in and we just dug them out of the ground and got the medical supplies out." Denius was awarded a second Silver Star for his efforts.

In January the 30th was caught up in a more famous German counteroffensive. Denius came out of it with a third Silver Star, a Purple Heart, and a trip back to England.

"We never called it 'The Battle of the Bulge,'" he says. "To us it was the Ardennes campaign—I got two purple hearts over there, but one was just a flesh wound that did not require evacuation. This time, in Belgium, I took shrapnel in the leg and also had severely frozen feet. They flew me back to England, and I spent three weeks in the hospital and then one week [of] rehab, and then rejoined my unit. It wasn't a 'million-dollar wound.'"

Then, as the 30th rolled through Germany, Denius once again found himself in a situation where, "the infantry unit I was supporting came under heavy fire from tanks and infantry. I was able to remain in my forward observation post and direct fire to stop the attack." He was awarded his fourth Silver Star.

"We kept going until we reached Magdeburg, on the Elbe River," he says. "And that's where we were when the cease-fire was ordered. By that time I had been offered a battlefield commission, but it would have meant leaving my division … and I wasn't about to leave those guys that I fought all that way with. Later, I was approved for OCS, but by that time the war was over, and I just came home."

Initially, however, coming home was not so simple. There was still a war going on in the Pacific. "Eventually they sent us back to Southhampton, England, and in early August we started boarding the Queen Mary for the trip home—but only for a 30-day leave. After that, we were to report to Camp Lewis, Washington, for amphibious training, for the invasion of Japan, but by the time we got back to the states, they had dropped the bombs on Hiroshima and Nagasaki, and it was over."

In March 1946, a colonel who had been appointed by Eisenhower as historian for the European Theatre of Operations and instructed to compile an exhaustive report on the performance of all combat units submitted his final report to his commanding general. After citing several units for commendation, the report continued:

> However, we picked the 30th Division No. 1 on the first category of infantry divisions. It was the combined judgment of the approximately 35 historical officers who had worked on the records and in the field that the 30th merited this distinction. It was our finding that the 30th had been outstanding in three operations and that we could consistently recommend it for citation on any one of these three occasions. It was further found that it had in no single instance performed discreditably or weakly when considered against the averages of the Theatre, and that in no single operation had it carried less than its share of the burden or looked bad when compared with the forces on its flanks. We were especially impressed with the fact that it had consistently achieved results without undue wastage of its men.
>
> I do not know whether further honors will come to the 30th. I hope they do for we had to keep looking at the balance of things always, and we felt that the 30th was the outstanding infantry division of the ETO.

Serving with the 30th Infantry, Denius says, "was kind of a 'Band of Brothers' type thing. But when I came back, I put those years behind me. I never relived them. I never talked about the war much to my family or anyone else, but when that movie, *Saving Private Ryan* came out ... there were a lot of people who knew I'd been in the war and brought it up. I've been asked about it more since then than in all those years before. I even went to see the movie with a friend of mine, another veteran, and we enjoyed it."

He is also aware of Tom Brokaw's book, and the prevailing notion that he and his comrades were the heroes of the last "good war."

Denius smiles.

"There's no such thing as a good war," he says. "As for us being the 'greatest generation,' I don't know if we were or not. I've never really given it much thought. But we did what we had to do ... when we had to do it."

Coming back from the war, Denius enrolled at UT at a time when the Longhorn football team featured the likes of Bobby Layne, Hub Bechtol, and Tom Landry. It was a great time to be a Longhorn, and Denius' life has carried a burnt orange hue ever since.

In December 1956, after Darrell Royal was hired to rescue the football program from utter despair, Denius paid the new coach a visit. "I had just been nominated as the Texas Exes counselor from the Austin area," he says, "and I asked Darrell if he would speak at our March 2 program, and I also told him I was interested in coming to the practices. We became friends almost immediately.

"I started showing up at practice, we got to know each other, pretty soon our families became friends, and we all just hit it off real well. His daughter babysat for our son. His oldest son went water skiing with us. Pretty soon we started getting together after the games. My wife is a great cook, and she would fix banana waffles. Darrell and I started playing chess—sitting there at the kitchen table while the wives were fixing the waffles—and it just got to be a regular thing.

"It's been just a great friendship. I still call him my coach."

Over the years, a close relationship with the UT coach has become a Denius tradition. "The ones who have followed Darrell in that job— Fred Akers, David McWilliams, John Mackovic, Mack Brown—I've had a great relationship with each of them, and it's really been a unique experience. I've stood on the sidelines at games, traveled with the team, gotten to know players and their families. It's been great."

Last fall, Denius attended his 60th straight Texas-OU game, blessedly witnessing the end of a five-year losing streak in the series. "Oklahoma has had some great teams in that span," he says, "but last year I felt going in that we were the dominant team, and after Billy Pittman caught that big pass just before the half, we were on a roll."

Denius then ponders the question of whether the famous rivalry's days at the Cotton Bowl are numbered. "I hope not," he says. "It's a fabulous classic—great for our fans and great for OU fans. It gives OU tremendous exposure to Texas [athletes]; it's an easy trip for both schools. It brings a lot of money into Dallas. I really hope they can find the means to renovate the stadium and keep it in Dallas.

"If you talk about home-and-home, you're talking about 4,000 OU fans coming to Austin one year and 4,000 UT fans going up there the next. You take away the unique aspect of the game and the spectacle of a packed stadium half orange and half red. It's like driving down a West Texas highway in the summer, where you can see the heat rising up off the pavement. When you go into the Cotton Bowl for Texas-OU, you can see the enthusiasm rising up out of the stands."

For Denius, the trip to Ohio State was one of the most memorable of his life.

"I hadn't seen my old radio sergeant, Sherman Goldstein, since May of 1945," he says. "He lives in Toledo and he's four years older than me. We talk on the phone and send cards each Christmas, but we had not seen each other in 60 years. The night before the game in Columbus, he drove down from Toledo, and we met again at last. We went to a great restaurant, and Bill Little from the university was in there with some media people. He steered them our way, and they all came over to talk to the two old veterans. Then the manager came around and told us everything was on the house.

"What a great reunion."

At 81, Denius presents the aspect of a much younger man, partly because, he says, "I got into exercise and physical fitness back in the fifties, when it wasn't really in vogue, and I've always had a lot of energy.

"I enjoy working … I enjoy practicing law. I have a wonderful family that I love, and I love the University of Texas—I have gained so much in life, personally, professionally, and socially from that connection.

"Hopefully, I can continue in good health and keep going to the practices and the games. I have no plans to retire."

3

Alumni of the Year

When Rick Gump began to channel his law practice toward the area of immigration and international business years ago, he and his wife, Diana, began to experience broadened horizons.

"One time," she recalls, "we had this Chinese family over for dinner at our house. I think they had only been in the country a day or two, and we wanted to make them feel welcome. I wasn't real sure what I could serve that they would want to eat, so I finally decided to just fix a simple, southern meal—brisket, fresh green beans, and homemade apple pie. In fact, the apples came from a tree in our backyard. I was a little apprehensive—just hoping they would like it—and they ate it all, every bite—parents and children alike. And when it was over, one of the little boys said, 'Oh, Mrs. Gump, you did better than McDonald's.'"

She took it as a high compliment, and this year the Gumps received another cherished accolade when they were named Alumni of the Year by the Dallas chapter of the Texas Exes. The award is befitting of the couple, since it encompasses the two entities they have spent their lives support-ing—their hometown and their alma mater.

Both 58, they met as sophomores at Thomas Jefferson High School and became instant sweethearts. They went to the University of Texas together and then returned to Dallas. Married 38 years, they have raised two children and remained active in the Longhorn Foundation and in civic roles locally.

A successful attorney for nearly 35 years, Rick has had his own prac-tice since 1985 and admits that, "So far, it's been a great ride."

The sentiment seems particularly relevant for Diana, because there was a time, long ago, when her present life seemed highly unlikely. By the time she got out of high school, she had had two tumors removed from her body, and life was not exactly looking like a slice of homemade apple pie.

"When I was four years old I had a cancer," she says. "It's called a Whilm's Tumor and it was on my kidney. So, they took the kidney out and got rid of the tumor. From then on, I was really healthy until I was 17—that's when the second one appeared, right at the start of my senior year in high school. This one was on the adrenal gland sitting above the [other] kidney. They told me they were both embryonic tumors. I'm just weird."

The second one caused a slightly larger problem than the first. "Some records got mixed up, and they weren't really sure which side it was on," she says. "So now I have two darts [incision scars], each more than a foot long running down my back."

As it turned out, she had a kidney removed from one side and the adrenal gland taken from the other, so she has never been required to take medication.

Diana's senior year in high school was less than enthralling.

"I had Cushing's disease—a benign tumor, but it caused some problems," she says. "You get the symptoms that I would describe as being like the Fat Lady in the circus. I had to shave to go to my senior prom, but [Rick] was right there beside me. A really good guy."

The tumor was removed right after graduation, in early June, but Diana still had problems. "The doctors encouraged me to lay out of school for at least a semester," she says, "and told me that I really needed to take a whole year off to regain my strength. But I had signed up for 12 hours—and at that age, you really want to get back in the swing of things, but it was hard. After something like that, it's hard to get your self-confidence back, and pretty soon I was ready to drop out of college."

But as Rick says, "She's a trooper—it was hard for her, and she had to go on scholastic probation, but she graduated in four years with a high academic standing and then got a job and taught school for two years until I got out of law school."

And so, she says, "When they honored us this year, I told people that I look back and think, 'Good Lord, if I had quit back then and given it all up, think of all the things I would have missed—all the things we love—and when they gave us that honor I thought, is this ever sweet.'"

Even before they met in sophomore biology class, Rick and Diana were on parallel courses in terms of at least one common interest. "My dad started taking me to football games when I was little," she says. "I had a cousin who played with Don Meredith at SMU. So I learned the game. When I met Rick, he invited me to a football game on the first date. He was real impressed that I understood the game and liked it."

Rick recalls that it was, "Thomas Jefferson and Highland Park—took her in my '56 Chevy."

A few weeks later, he took her to the '62 Texas-OU game. And, she says, when they went again in 1963—a decisive Texas victory in a show-down between the nation's two top-ranked teams—"I was hooked on the Horns forever."

Rick was already pretty much bleeding orange, since his father—also an attorney—and a sister had gone to UT. "My dad had been taking me to games all my life: Texas games, SMU games, Cotton Bowl games," he says. "But when I was a high school junior in 1963 and Texas won the national championship, it really got to be a big thing. Down the stretch that year, he actually took me out of classes a few times so we could make it to Austin or wherever they were playing and watch the game. We ended up sitting in the Cotton Bowl, watching them demolish Navy for the national championship."

In fact, gazing back through the mists, Gump to this day can still focus clearly on a four-day sequence in the fall of '63 that remains one of his fondest memories. "It started on Thursday night when Thomas Jefferson played Paschal, the powerhouse team from Fort Worth. They had a great team and we were just so-so, but we managed to pull an upset and beat them. Then on Friday night Navy came down to the Cotton Bowl and played SMU in what is still one of the greatest games I ever saw. Roger Staubach was great, but John Roderick had a great game for SMU, and they pulled off a big upset win, 32–28.

"On Saturday in the Cotton Bowl there was the Texas-OU game, and although [OU was] favored, we won big [28–7] and became the nation's No. 1 team in the rankings. I was back in the Cotton Bowl on Sunday, watching Dallas play Philadelphia. The Cowboys weren't winning back then, but they beat the Eagles that day. When it was over I thought, 'I've watched four great games in a row where my team won— in four straight days. This will never happen again.

"And it hasn't, but it was a fun streak."

As a senior at TJ, Gump was a cheerleader and played on the golf team, but by then he had another, more high-profile gig. While Diana was getting sick, Rick was living the high life as a Dallas Cowboys cheerleader. "I've always told people that I finally had to quit because my halter top kept falling off," he says.

It is a seldom-noted aspect of American history that, long before Tex Schramm came up with the brilliant entertainment ploy that forever transformed the ambience of NFL sidelines, the Cowboys had cheerleaders. They got them from local high schools, and Rick was one of them. "They had tryouts, and that's how you got on the team," he says. "It was fun, but we really weren't as popular as the ones they had later."

By that time, he was already a Cowboy fan. "My dad bought season tickets when they first came here in 1960," he says. " I can still walk you to the seats—Section 5, Row 25. We went to every single Cowboy game but one until I went off to college. We've been Cowboy fans ever since. In fact, when my parents were alive we'd go with them, and then when our kids came along we started taking them and just made it our Sunday outing. I really watch them more on TV now, although I did go to the '94 Super Bowl."

During four years at Forty Acres, the couple developed a deep love for the university whose football team they had cheered for so long, but the Gumps also knew they would come back and make their home in Dallas. "I got a degree in government in the spring of '69, and Diana got a degree in elementary education," Rick says. "We had gotten married in '68, but the Vietnam War was going on, and I had signed up for the reserves. Literally, the day you graduated, you had to go in the Army to do basic training for the reserves, and I was sent to Fort Bragg. I was trained to interrogate prisoners of war, but I got into a reserve unit because I could speak Spanish. People were scrambling like crazy to get into the reserves, and a language capability helped.

"I came back and did two and a half years in law school while Diana taught school, and graduated in December 1972. We had our trailer loaded and I dropped off my last paper at the law school and we headed for Dallas, and we've been here ever since."

Over the years since then, perhaps the singular oddity is that neither of their children went to UT. Travis, now 30, is a Baylor graduate and works for Homeland Security, while Jenny, 27, went to Stephen F. Austin and has completed her Master's in Psychology. "Well, for a lot of the time they were growing up, [the Longhorns] just weren't very good," Rick says. "There was a long dry spell in there."

Nevertheless, Rick and Diana kept going to the games—their season tickets are of an ancient vintage, going back to his father—and becoming involved in the Longhorn Foundation (Diana is on the Advisory Council) and the Texas Exes. After 13 years in the firm where his father was one of the founders, Rick went off on his own. Almost by chance at first, he also changed his focus from conventional business law to immigration.

"For a long time," he says, "I did bank formation, real estate, general business work, but one day there was a situation where a guy who was a professor at Kansas and was from China, decided he wanted to open a Chinese restaurant in Dallas, and he wanted to do it through one of the banks we had chartered. I came back from lunch and there was a book of Confucius' Sayings on my desk, and I was told that in about an hour three Chinese were coming in who wanted to open a restaurant, and they needed to immigrate.

"Nobody at the firm had a clue on how to do immigration work—least of all me—so I had to ask a lot of questions and figure it out. We ended up opening three restaurants and bringing chefs and investors in from China, and that's how it got started.

"When the banking and real estate work dried up in the mid-eighties, I decided to go full-bore on the international side, so now I do everything from work-site compliance and getting visas and citizenship for people and companies to strategic planning for international groups. It has been very satisfying. About three weeks ago, a mother and two of her children visited my office—people who have been clients of mine since the seventies. When they originally came here, all they could afford was one Volkswagen to haul the whole family around in.

"The father had been in the army and [in] the regime of Chiang Kai-shek, and was a very intelligent man. The teenage daughter was a very beautiful girl. She's 42 now and she's been a model for the Kim Dawson Agency and has been on the cover of *Texas Monthly* and many other magazines, and has been a judge at the Miss Universe Pageant. The brother now lives in Hong Kong and runs a multibillion dollar venture capital firm."

Meanwhile, for Rick and Diana, life in pursuit of Greater Longhorn Glory continues, although there's something floating in the wind right now they're not too crazy about—the talk of moving the Texas-OU game out of the Cotton Bowl and making it a home-and-home affair. "Since the first one he took me to in 1962, we've been to every one of those games but two," Diana says. "But you know we're not going up to

Oklahoma. At best, it would be every other year for us, when it's in Austin."

Rick agrees. "I think that for the history of that game, and obviously for the benefit of the city, it would be a travesty to see it moved—regardless of the financial issue that I totally understand. It's still the one game I know of that is a top game where you have the stadium full and divided in half amongst the opposing fans. It just really is fun."

Either way, the Gumps remain Longhorns forever. "We just loved it so much when we were there," he says. " We learned how to make a living and we had so much fun there; there's so much to do, so much to learn, so many friends you make, so many friends you meet later through the continuing connection—it has just always seemed right that we try to give something back. Diana is on the College of Education advisory council, and there are always things you can do.

"We just hope we can continue participating. It has been such a large part of our lives."

4

The Freshman Cheerleader

Lacey Taylor loves the University of Texas. And she also loves the city of Austin.

She loves Austin so much, in fact, that she named her dog after the town.

"I know, it's crazy," she says, laughing. "At first, I actually thought about naming him 'Bevo' or 'Texas' but I decided that was probably a little silly—actually, he's brown and white, not burnt orange. So I settled for 'Austin.'"

The obvious choice, actually.

A Houston native, Taylor can trace her love of UT and Austin precisely to August 1992, when her father brought her up for her first visit. She was instantly infatuated, despite the fact that all her friends were about to become, um, Aggies. She quickly became one of the first two incoming freshmen ever to make the UT cheerleading squad, but over the next few years her life took several unexpected turns.

Injuries forced her to give up the sport she loved, and other priorities eventually led her to leave Austin and finish her degree elsewhere. "I always said I'd be back," she says. But she never dreamed that 10 years later she would go to the Rose Bowl with another group of Longhorn cheerleaders and watch Texas win a national championship.

Now 30, Taylor is back "home" working as a pediatric nurse at the Children's Hospital of Austin and then going to her second job—helping to coach the current UT cheerleaders. "I have a great life right now and I'm having fun," she says. Not that the path from there to here was always exactly smooth. "Growing up in Houston, I was always a cheerleader," she says. "I started doing Little League when I was about 10, and it was always a part of my life.

"Up through my junior year in high school, I never thought much about where I wanted to go to college. My parents didn't go to college, and my grandfather went to LSU, so I thought I might do that ... but all [of] my friends were going to Texas A&M and—well, you know, peer pressure—I was just saying, 'Yeah, I'm going to A&M.'

"By the time I was a senior, I had decided I wanted to go into medicine, and I was leaning away from A&M. I wanted to go to a big school with a lot of tradition, and I sort of began focusing on the traditions of the different schools, and I was also thinking about cheerleading, so I decided to apply at Texas. I think it was just UT, the traditions, the whole city of Austin ... plus, they had cheerleaders. I got accepted, which was a good thing, because it's the only place I applied.

"My dad brought me for a visit to UT before my senior year in high school, and I said, 'This is what I want.'

"My dad said, 'Are you sure?' and I said, 'Absolutely.'"

"That was in August '92, and then later I decided to try out for cheerleader. It was kind of a last-minute, almost spur-of-the-moment thing, and it was actually a little scary, but I told myself, 'If you don't try it, then you'll never know, and you'll probably regret it.' That was the first year they let incoming freshmen try out—you could try out if you were a freshman already in school, but they had never let the ones just coming in do it. They were going to take one male and one female, so I trained and trained and trained and got my skills up and made it. My friend, John Kulasa, became the first male and I was the first female."

For Taylor, it opened up an experience that has stayed with her ever since. "It was amazing; a great experience," she says, "especially for a freshman.

"I met a group of people I still keep in contact with. I don't see them as much as I would like, because we're kind of scattered, but I got an e-mail from one of the girls saying they were organizing a group to go on vacation together. We also formed a tailgate group. It's called the Texas Tailgaters. Over the years it has grown with people's families, but it was originally a Texas cheerleaders group.

"As for the experience itself, it was the neatest thing. It was amazing to me how much impact you can have on young people; little girls and boys who get so thrilled if you spend time with them and make them feel special.

"I remember the first time I walked out on the field at Memorial Stadium I was really stunned, cheering for that many people, and actually having everyone yell.

"Even today, when I go out on the field and hear everyone yell, 'Texas Fight' it still gives me the chills. It's crazy … just a great feeling that you can't describe. I tell my cheerleaders now, 'Cherish this moment, it's one you will never forget—all the people up in the stands, yelling, holding up their horns, just the passion that you see up there.'"

Taylor performed for a year and a half, and then saw things come to an abrupt end.

"I made the team my second year," she says, "but by that time I was having shoulder problems, and it was just too hard to do a lot of the skills when I was hurt. I couldn't tumble, and there are routines where you have to do a flip, and it was just hard. It was kind of a wear-and-tear thing. I had had several dislocations in high school, and if you just keep stressing it and don't let it heal it's a continual problem. So I was about at the point where I was thinking I needed to take a break and let things heal.

"Also, into my second year, I was kind of asking, 'What do I want to do with my life?' and feeling the need to focus more on my grades and just going through a transition period. But I still loved cheerleading, and when my coach came around and told me I had made the travel squad for the first road game up at Pitt, I was just so excited. Then, in practice that week, I dislocated my shoulder again and couldn't go.

"It just killed me. They had a great trip—got to meet Tony Dorsett, had a wonderful time—and to this day, there is a picture of all of them on that trip hanging in the cheerleader office. It just kills me. But my shoulders just weren't doing right, and it was time to look at something else. I was offered a job in the office, organizing travel, keeping in touch with the cheerleaders, and I took it. The thought of leaving was hard, because those people were my whole life. I wasn't in a sorority, and they were my group."

In the midst of this, Taylor changed majors. "I had been focusing on maybe medicine or child development, and then I just decided to go into pediatric nursing," she says. "I had to start all over.

"I got accepted here at UT, and I was all excited, and then my stepmother became pregnant—she had been with us since I was four, and she and my father had tried for 16 years. When the time finally came, my little brother was born early. He's great now—10 years old and taller than me—but at the time there were medical bills, and I decided to move back home to save money.

"My dad had spoiled me, paying for everything all those years, and I decided to do the right thing—take responsibility and be an adult. So I moved home and finished up at UT-Galveston. But I always told my parents, 'Someday, I'm going back to Austin.'"

In 1999, she graduated with a Bachelor of Science degree in science and nursing, and then spent three years in Houston doing pediatric nursing at Herman's Children's Hospital. "I felt that was the best place for me," she says, "because I eventually wanted to go into ER pediatric nursing. When the opportunity came up to move back to Austin, I contacted the ER here at the children's hospital and got a job. I also phoned a friend of mine who is the cheerleading coach at UT and told him I was coming back, and he asked me to coach. So I moved back to

Austin in 2002 and started practicing nursing and coaching again. The contrast between ER and coaching is greatly relaxing and kind of gives me a release when I need it."

Along with these changes, Taylor had a disappointing personal relationship—a four-year romance that suddenly evaporated. "He was a guy I knew at UT," she says. "We ran into each other again, started dating, got engaged, bought a car together, bought a house together, lived in it for four months, and then he had a change of heart. You live and learn."

The upside was that she was back in Austin. "There's no place like Austin," she says. "You have all these people of different backgrounds living together in harmony. You have the legislative people, you have the hippies, you have the college students, and they all just kind of hang out together with no problem. It's a fantastic place."

This time, being part of the cheerleading contingent at UT came with a bonus that could be considered just compensation for that long-ago lost trip to Pittsburgh:

The Rose Bowl.

"It was so much fun," she says. "I went out with the cheerleaders. We left on New Year's Eve on a chartered flight with the band—so we had 400 band members, 16 cheerleaders, plus eight dancers and the mascots, because we're actually the spirit program, which includes mascots and dancers, but I just coach the cheerleaders. We left early that day and got there around eight in the morning and just relaxed the rest of the day—kind of looking around, getting some rest, and [went on] some planned activities. We went to Universal Studios and some other things. The next day we went sightseeing and the bus driver showed us around Los Angeles, and we went to Disney and did the rides."

The real fun came the next day. You probably have to be a Longhorn to understand this:

"The next day was the Parade of Roses," Taylor says. We got up at 4 a.m. to meet on the bus at five, and it is raining and freezing cold. We're out there, it is 53 degrees, raining, and all the kids have their ponchos on, and the coaches are out there in jeans and sneakers and ponchos. By the time we start the parade it starts really pouring down rain— the parade is like five miles. We were soaked from head to toe … but it was just the best time. We were not even a third of the way through and our kids are like, 'OK, let's have some fun.' They pulled back their hoods, they were soaking wet, hair was soaked, pom poms were soaked—but the crowd was great, even though the majority were USC fans, and we were marching through the crowd holding up our horns … it was really fun. The only problem was that by the end of the parade you were so cold you couldn't hold your horns up anymore. You just couldn't form the sign with your fingers.

'I've got the greatest pictures—at the end, our float was melting. It just disintegrated. After that, we just kinda took it easy for the rest of the day."

The next day was filled with public appearances. And then it was January 4. "It was really beautiful out there," she says. "We had a pep rally and then went to the tailgate. What a tailgate—it was just huge, and I saw several people I knew, and it was really incredible. There were people out there who didn't have tickets to the game but flew out there to support the Longhorns.

"Then, of course, the game itself was phenomenal. The crowd was amazing—that's the loudest Texas crowd I've ever heard, and then when we were down for a while, it got real quiet and I got scared."

Taylor's fears were ultimately relieved because, "At the end, people who didn't even know each other were crying and hugging.

"The next day, we went to Disneyland with the band, then flew home. By the time we got home, it was 4 a.m. on the sixth. It was freezing cold, but driving up on the bus, you could see the tower lit up orange and it was so exciting to see that big number one up there.

"Awesome.

"Now I'm just enjoying life in Austin and with my two jobs. I've gotten to where I refer to the cheerleaders as my children. And a new children's hospital is supposed to be ready in 2007, and I'm aiming getting my Masters degree and teaching nursing at UT.

"I just love being here, and I hope I can live here the rest of my life."

5

Texas' Biggest Fans

If you are looking for a certain residence in the Pleasant Grove section of Dallas, there really is no need to cruise along, scanning the street numbers printed on the curb. Just follow the directions, and when you turn a corner, your destination will suddenly become clear to you. At a glance, it seems to resemble a gingerbread house ... except that the operable color is definitely colored burnt orange.

The sign above the door reads: "Texas' Biggest Fans ... Radar and Lila."

Above the garage is another sign, proclaiming it "Longhorn Country."

In the front of the house, there is a large ceramic model of the state of Texas, and next to it stands a very large Longhorn made of solid cement.

Inside you will find Radar and Lila Thomas—71 and 83, respectively—up to their ears in Longhorn memorabilia.

They bought the house in 1971, but over the years with their growing collection and extensive wardrobes, they have partially outgrown it. Most—but not all—of their collection now sits in an additional room they had built onto the house in 1988. "It actually cost twice what we paid for the house," Radar says, "but that's largely a reflection of the change in real estate values."

Lila notes, "We would have made it bigger, but there's a tree behind it in the back yard that I didn't want cut down."

To enter it is to feel the breath of Bevo. There are countless caps, hats, cups, glasses, plates, shirts, jackets, photos, banners, magazines, books, newspaper clippings, boots, belt buckles, rugs, floor mats, wall hangings, pens, pencils, and furniture items—all in the appropriate color and bearing some form of UT insignia. There is a Longhorn mailbox and a roll of Longhorn toilet paper. There are Longhorns made out of pecans and Longhorns made out of tree stumps. There is a large glass Longhorn and one that lights up.

There is a Longhorn telephone that Lila bought in 1973. For over 30 years, she has paid $5 every three months to rent it. "It's from a novelty store, and they won't let you buy it," she says. "I can't believe I've been paying on it all this years, but if you've gotta have it ..."

There is a Longhorn Christmas tree, and an orange golf bag, although Radar no longer plays golf. There are Longhorn wastebaskets, chairs, benches, and desks. There is replica of the Texas Tower, which Radar lights up orange after every win.

There are complete volumes of *Texas Football Magazine* and a half-dozen UT publications and a program from a UT football game played in 1927. There are programs from every home game since 1977—when the couple bought season tickets—until last year, when they missed a few games.

In one corner sits a plaque that reads, "If God Isn't a Longhorn, Why is the Sunset Burnt Orange?" In another corner sits a photo of a great-grandson who Radar swears has burnt orange hair. "He's 19 now," he says, "but when he was little, people used to come up and tell him he had beautiful red hair, and he would get mad and say, 'It's not red—it's burnt orange!' And really, it still is."

There is Radar's pride and joy—a pair of orange boots with a Longhorn stitched on one side and 'Radar' on the other. Lila's pride and joy is a book that she has filled since 1981 with autographs of players and coaches, as well as signatures from players who go back as far as 1941. There is a certificate of gratitude for the services of "Coach Radar Thomas, 1980" recalling the day he spent on the sideline as a guest coach. Lifetime, he's 0-1.

It's the work of a lifetime and a work of love that began long ago, in Amarillo. "I was actually born in Clarendon, but we moved to Amarillo when I was a year old," Radar says. He was the son of John Melvin and Effie Thomas and given the name John Melvin Jr., but unless you have a copy of his driver's license, you would never know it. From the time he was a little boy, people called him Radar, and virtually no one has known him otherwise. "We used to have friends who complained that they couldn't call us because we weren't in the phone book," Lila says. "We were in there, but they didn't know where to look, and finally we had to have it listed as Radar."

As Radar recalls, "I started out selling papers when I was a little boy, and I had real big ears. I used to pull on them and that made them big, I guess. Or that's what my mother said. One day I was walking down the street and these two old pressmen were sitting there on a bench, and they said, 'Look, here comes Radar.' And it stuck.

"My father worked bottling Dr. Pepper for 27 years there. Back during the Depression, he had helped build the Hoover Dam. He and my mother had 10 kids—eight girls—and after I finished the 11th grade, I quit school and went to work to help my mother as much as I could.

"Eventually I went to work as a pressman for the Amarillo paper, and I worked there 18 years until we had a strike. We lost, so I came on down to Dallas and worked in the pressroom of the *Morning News* for 27 years. We also had a strike there and lost, and I was off for about a year, but two of my foremen wanted me back real bad, so I went back and stayed. I retired in 1995."

The daughter of W. D. and Ora Thurman, Lila grew up in the Depression and graduated from Amarillo High in 1940. "I was a fan of the Amarillo Sandies back when there wasn't anything else," she says. "My daddy had a shoe repair shop for about 40 years and had a heart attack. My mother only went through the third grade in school, but she later taught herself to type and worked at the hospital for 20 years. The thing I remember most growing up, was all those dust storms we had. It was so odd—you could stand there and watch them coming, and it was so quiet. Then all of a sudden all that black dirt settled ... and you couldn't even see the light in the house."

Her courtship with Radar, she says, also seemed a little odd, at first. "When I met him," she says, "I was divorced and had three kids and was working as a waitress at a place where he and some of the pressmen would come in on the night shift. I was dating his best friend, but then he left. The three of us were together a lot, so when Radar asked me to go to a movie, I didn't think much about it. We were friends.

"Then one day he asked me to marry him, and I said, 'It isn't going to work—I have a son, 12, a daughter, 10, and another daughter, 5, and I'm 11 years older than you are. This will not work.' So now we've been married 51 years, and he's still trying to make it work."

By the time they were married, Radar had become a Longhorn fan. "I'm not really sure how it happened," he says, "When I was a kid I wanted to go down there and play for Texas, but I knew I wasn't big enough. So I said, 'By golly, I'll just become a big Longhorn fan.' I think I also kind of had the feeling that it was the state school of Texas, and if I was going to be a Texan, I needed to be a fan of the university.

"I was also a big fan of the Brooklyn Dodgers, while they were still in Brooklyn. When they moved to California, I lost interest, but I remember me and some of the guys I knew used to sit out in the car and drink beer and listen to the Texas games on the radio. Sometimes we would drive over when they played in Fort Worth or Dallas and watch the game."

The first game Radar and Lila saw together had no Longhorns in it. "It was right after we were married," she says, "He said he always wanted to go to the Cotton Bowl, and I said 'Let's go,' and he said, 'That's silly—that game's sold out every year, and you can't get tickets.' So I wrote a letter to somebody at the Cotton Bowl, saying how wonderful my husband was and he had married me with three kids, and all he was asking from life was to go to the Cotton Bowl, and did they have four tickets I could buy, because we had to have friends come with us. We wound up with four tickets. We didn't get four together, but the other couple was only two rows up from us. I'll never forget—it was the Dicky Maegle game."

Or, as the Dicky Maegle legend is known to posterity, the January 1, 1954, Cotton Bowl game between Rice and Alabama in which Crimson Tide captain Tommy Lewis became nationally famous and eternally shamed for lurching off the bench to tackle Maegle—Rice's star half-back—who was en route to a 95-yard scoring run. In the aftermath, Maegle was awarded the balance of the run and led the Owls to a 28–6 triumph. Lewis was mortified, both he and Maegle appeared on the *Ed Sullivan Show*, and Lila was amazed. "I remember shouting, 'That guy was sitting on the bench and now he's tackling that other guy!'" she says, laughing. "Funniest game I ever saw."

Years later, when Radar's job situation necessitated the move to Dallas, the couple turned themselves into serious Longhorn fans. They soon bought the house in Pleasant Grove and began collecting all things orange—including cars. "For about 20 years, I had an orange Vega," Radar says, and for several years Lila drove an orange Nova with a white top. Both cars had "Hook 'em Horns painted on the side and a horn that played "The Eyes of Texas."

Radar and Lila became season-ticket holders in '77 and began traveling the world with the Longhorns to places such as Georgia, Alabama, The Meadowlands at Penn State, Stanford, Hawaii, and Provo, Utah—in addition to the locales in the Southwest Conference. By 1980, the couple had become so prominent and popular that Lila got a strange phone call. "They said it was Fred Akers calling, and he wanted to talk to Radar," she says. "I thought it was a joke, but I got a return number and sure enough, it was his office. They wanted Radar to come down and be a guest coach.

"At the next home game, I had to fend for myself while [Radar] got to eat lunch with the players and be in there watching them get taped, and then stand on the sidelines all day, and go in at halftime and listen to the pep talk from the coaches."

Unfortunately, the opponent that day was SMU in its "Pony Express" heyday, and the Longhorns went down to defeat, "That hurt," he says, "I was just so disappointed, but it was still an experience I will always cherish."

Over the years, however, there were a couple of engagements at the Cotton Bowl that were not quite as festive as the Dicky Maegle game.

"One year we went to the OU game," Lila recalls, "and we went into the pregame tailgate place there, and they had mixed drinks and barbeque, so I had them fix me a Crown and Seven and some barbeque. I took one sip and one bite … and started throwing up and throwing up and throwing up. They took me into the emergency area there, and I remember hearing them saying, 'We're losing her! We're losing her! … Transport! Transport!' and they got ready to take me to Baylor Hospital."

Like a loyal Longhorn trooper, she instructed the remaining member of the group to carry on. "I told Radar, 'They're taking me to Baylor— you go on and go to the game. Don't worry about me. But he got in the ambulance and went to the hospital with me, and we both missed the game. There wasn't even a TV set there for him to watch. I was sick as a dog all night, but they released me the next morning without ever declaring what it was. A touch of food poisoning, I expect."

The second instance involved the Cotton Bowl game itself. "I had this thing on my leg that the doctor said was just a cyst," she says, "But it swelled up the day of the game, and we had my granddaughter visiting from South Carolina, and I told them to just go on. I said just turn on the TV and give me the newspaper and phone, and I'll be OK, but after everybody left I got sick and started vomiting, and it just kept getting worse and worse. After the game they called because they were going on to some friends' house for a party, and I said, 'Oh, I'm just fine, you go ahead.' By the time they got back they could hardly get me out of the bed, and that time I spent three weeks in the hospital with a staph infection."

Worse things could happen, of course. "One year for the A&M game, we went over to College Station on a bus," Lila says, "but for some reason, our seats weren't in the same place as everyone else's and we ended up sitting with a bunch of Aggies. We were wearing orange, but we were nice to everyone, and when the game ended we got up to leave, then these two big old Aggies got up and blocked our way and said, 'You're not leaving until we say you can leave our stadium.' "And we said, 'But we have a bus to catch,' and they said, 'Well, that's too bad.'" After a few words between Radar and the two Aggies, the situation diffused and everyone went home. It has left Radar, however, with a rather uncharitable view of the hosts. "A&M," he says, "As far as I'm concerned … stands for Assholes and Morons."

He has a more kindly view of the Big Red people from up north of the river—but only because of the usual suspect. "Darrell Royal is the best Oklahoma boy I ever saw," he says, grinning. "To hell with the rest of 'em, but I do love DKR."

Once you get way up into Arkansas, Lila says, the people are actually rather charming. "When I got my little orange Nova in '77," she says, "we drove it up there on a little vacation. People always said, 'Don't go to Arkansas—you can't buy gas if you're from Texas', and all that stuff, but we went up there and did sightseeing and shopping and the whole bit, with me dressed in orange and all that good stuff, and everything was fine. Finally, we stopped at a little curio shop and when we came back out—draped across my windshield was a big banner that read, 'You're in Razorback Country.' They didn't stick it on or anything, just draped it across the windshield, and I thought that was kind of cute. The whole trip, everyone was real nice to us."

Then the couple took a trip to Brigham Young; definitely a different place. "They had a nonsmoking stadium long before others did," Lila says. "We had a friend who went with us and she smoked, but she knew it was a no-smoking stadium, so she had these little fake cigarettes that you don't light but you just hold them in your hand. They evicted her. She protested and said, 'These aren't real cigarettes.' They told her she couldn't bring anything into the stadium that even looked like a cigarette, and threw her out."

Some of the best trips, however, were excursions to antique shops, flea markets, and garage sales. Radar and Lila's horde of Texas treasure kept increasing, and led them, eventually, to the arrival of the cement Longhorn adorning their front yard. "We were driving over near Forney on our way to a flea market," Radar says, "when I glanced over to the side of the road and said, 'Looky-there, honey, there's a concrete Longhorn!' So, we turned around and went back, but we found out it was $350, and we couldn't afford it."

Nevertheless, when Radar retired from the newspaper a short time later, the $350 suddenly appeared. "My coworkers took up a collection and gave it to me, so we went back and bought it," he says.

Radar soon discovered that he and retirement were not a good fit— "I couldn't stand just sitting around doing nothing"—so he got a job at a local Tom Thumb store and worked another five years.

His only complaint now is that he can no longer go to the OU game. "It used to be that if you had season tickets you could get tickets to that game," he says, "but now you have to have big money to do that, and I just don't have it. In a way, it kind of breaks my heart, because I bleed orange and I can't get the tickets, but I still watch it on TV. It's not the same, but at least I can watch it."

Lila's daughters—Glenda and Artie—grew up, raised families, and are currently living in Amarillo and Martindale. Her son, Dewey, died in a parachute accident at age 43 in 1988. "He also worked at the [Dallas] paper, in the mailroom," she says. "It was his hobby—he had made over

900 jumps, so it's not like he was a novice or anything. [He was] doing free falls, and he just didn't open his chute in time."

Lila is still collecting signatures in her book, which contains a special notation by the name of Chris Samuels. "One time we went to a big road game—I think it may have been at Auburn," she says, "and all of the players were upstairs in their rooms and I was kind of hesitant about going up there, and Chris offered to take the book upstairs and get the autographs. "He was gone a long time, and finally I thought, 'Well, there goes my book,' but he finally came back and he had gotten every single player on the team to sign it.

"So I wrote a note by his signature that says, 'Very nice boy.'

"Another time, David McWilliams was up here in Dallas and he took my book back to Austin and got everyone on the team to sign it, and then mailed it back to me."

Assessing what these 50-odd years of faithfully following and supporting the Texas Longhorns has meant, Radar is able to condense the thought into a single word.

"Life," he says.

Elaborating on that a bit, Lila says, "When I worked [as a bookkeeper at M&M Food Stores], we always arranged my vacations so we could travel with the team. I've seen the Statue of Liberty and I've been to California and Hawaii, and if it hadn't been for all this I probably would have never left the state of Texas.

"Really, I don't think we would have had much of a life if we hadn't had the Longhorns."

6

50ᵗʰ Anniversary Surprise

When Jack and Joyce Gerrick noticed their 50th wedding anniversary rolling into view, they gave it some careful thought and then did the normal thing. They took a cruise. Many couples tend to celebrate anniversaries this way, especially if one of them—Joyce—is a travel agent.

"We took a beautiful 11-day cruise, had a great time, came back home to Fort Worth, and figured that was that," she says.

On the following Monday—the actual anniversary—events strayed towards the abnormal. Their kids—Mark and Gayle—had a little something extra in mind.

"The deal was, we were supposed to meet the kids for brunch at Colonial Country Club," Joyce says. "We didn't see them when we got there, but I saw a friend of mine, Sandra Lusker, in the lobby and I went over to talk to her. She knows everybody, and I was telling her that I badly needed to get an invitation to the Davey O'Brien Award dinner, because I really wanted to meet Vince Young and shake his hand and congratulate him on such a wonderful season and career. She said, 'There are some people in this room over here who could probably help you— they're having a private party in there.'

"I said, 'I can't go into a private party,' but she sort of drug me in there." Joyce Gerrick opened the door, and was met with the usual greeting:

"Surprise!"

Inside were all of the Gerricks' old friends … and a few extras. For starters, Darrell Royal was there—brought up from Austin in a limousine arranged by Mark and Gayle. A fair smattering of Longhorn immortality presented themselves as well, including Cotton Speyrer, Pat Culpepper, Billy Dale, David and Paul Kristynik, Todd Dodge, Blake Brockermeyer, and Calvin Shiraldi.

"There must have been 100 people in there, with orange and white decorations and Longhorn balloons," Joyce says. "Jack and I were in total shock. They have pictures of me with my mouth dropped open. David Kristynik works with my son and helped arrange it. We sang 'The Eyes of Texas' at the end, and it was just such a terrific thing to meet all those people and talk to them. I still can't believe it. Now I have an autographed photo of Darrell Royal."

The arrangement was a fitting gift for Joyce, an Alabama native who fell in love with the University of Texas while a student there in the fifties. She met and married Jack (now retired from the mattress business), had two children—"Longhorns," she says—and spent 25 years sitting behind Hub Bechtol at UT football games.

Eventually she entered the travel business, and for the past 20 years has served as the unofficial travel agent for Longhorn fans looking to follow the football team on the road. On her most recent adventure, she shepherded nearly 50 local Longhorns at the Rose Bowl. "This is just a sideline," says Gerrick, who works at Sanders Travel Center in Fort Worth. "Most of the year I book real trips for real people. This is just a lot of fun. It started about 25 years ago, when I was looking for something to do and wound up going to travel school. I worked several years at three other agencies and then came over here when Robin Sanders opened this office.

"The way it started was that after I was working in a travel office, people started calling and asking about trips to Longhorn games. Since I was usually going to the game anyway, I thought, 'Why not take them along?' I started putting trips together for people I knew—Longhorn fans. I didn't advertise. I was just doing it on my own; by word of mouth. The thing just kept building, and now it's just a large group of people that go to the games together."

The trips are for road games—most Longhorn fans can find their own way to Austin—and normally for excursions that are too long for a bus ride. The cost is reasonable and the objective is to have fun and share camaraderie among die-hard Longhorn fans. Gerrick has qualified as one since Dwight Eisenhower was in the White House, yet seems to find it strange that not everybody is that way.

When the pilot of the plane—a Texas Tech grad, as it happened— flying the Rose Bowl group back home was insufficiently solicitous of Texas' national championship, she says, "I had a few words with him."

Joyce grew up in Birmingham and says she never considered going to Alabama because it was "Just too close to home." She visited Illinois and was not impressed. "I really didn't know where I wanted to go," she says, "but I ran into somebody who had gotten out of high school ahead of me and gone to Texas, and they said, 'This is a great school.'

"So I applied, got in, went there without ever having set foot on campus, got started ... and I loved it. I met Jack, and after we got married and graduated from UT, we moved to Alabama for six years. Both of my kids were born there. But then he took a job with a mattress company [Sealy] in Fort Worth, and we've been here ever since. Once the kids were old enough we started going down to the games, and we finally got season tickets that someone had given up, and we were going to all the games. When I got into the travel business, it just seemed like kind of a natural development to start the trips.

"My trips are minimally priced and done through this agency, and have nothing to do with the Longhorn Foundation. A lot of times people will do their own air, and I will do hotel reservations and arrange buses to the stadiums. Other times I will block out seats on a flight and handle the whole thing."

When the Gerricks attend games, Bob Turpin, a trusted companion, usually accompanies them. On the surface, Turpin appears to be an inoffensive, completely rational real estate sales man. However, when confronted with distressing news about the Longhorns—or perhaps an unflattering opinion thereof—he becomes rather surly. He is normally quite personable, even charming, but there are those who would suggest that he needs to be watched closely.

Among those are the umpires from the league where he once coached a Little League baseball team—who, he admits, "advised me to take tranquilizers before each game."

Turpin retains a vivid memory of the 1961 TCU game—in which the underdog Horned Frogs pulled off a stunning 6–0 upset, which eventually stood as the only blemish on what might have been a national championship season for the Longhorns. "I've hated TCU ever since," he says. "All those years afterward when we were still in the same conference, every time we played TCU I got sick."

He's had even worse luck with Arkansas—there was a game up there back in the sixties, he recalls, where the Hog fans were so impressed with him that "after the game, they told me I'd better get out of Arkansas real fast."

Then, a few years later, there was the attempt to mend his ways. "I was a banker before I got into real estate," he says, "and a guy I worked with in the office was a big Arkansas fan, but we were good friends, so we decided to go together and take our wives—my first wife, actually—up to the game. But by the time it was over, we weren't such good friends anymore. My wife and his wife got into a fight, and after that things were a little tense around the office."

There was also that infamous affair in 1981. The Longhorns—coming off a thrashing of Oklahoma—were undefeated and ranked No. 1 in the nation, until they crashed in Arkansas. The final score was 42–11 and the collateral damage was spectacular. "I was just so upset," Turpin says. "I had a date that night, and we were cooking steaks—I'd had quite a few drinks—and I was fixing the steaks and I just kept thinking about the game and I got more and more upset, and all of a sudden I just took the knife and stabbed the steak as hard as I could. Unfortunately, my hand slipped down the blade, and pretty soon there was blood everywhere. I don't think I ever saw that woman again."

There have been better days, of course. Turpin says he "got a lot of gloating in" when he worked at a Midland bank—among Tech fans—during UT's 30-game winning streak years ago. "And at the Ohio State game this year," he says, "we tailgated with several members of their 1968 national championship team, and it was a lot of fun, and I enjoyed meeting them. But even today, I can't sleep when we lose—may as well not even try. I think this is something that has just kept building up with me, and it gets worse every year. When we lose now, my wife basically just doesn't talk to me."

Turpin's most redeeming quality, however, is that he has very clear vision—which over the years has been a comfort to Gerrick, who shields her eyes when the Longhorns are in a moment of crisis. "I just can't watch," she says. "This has been going on for years. ... I can watch the game as long as we're ahead, but when something potentially bad is happening, Bob has to stand beside me and tell me what's going on. I missed the winning field goal against Michigan in the Rose Bowl, even though I was sitting right there in the end zone where it happened. And this year against USC, he basically had to describe the last six minutes to me."

The routine has even been extended to some televised games in the Gerrick home, where, Turpin says, "if a crisis comes up, she'll go stand in the hallway."

Nevertheless, regarding those games where she may have missed part of the action, Joyce says, "Yeah, but at least I was there."

For most of the past 25 years, Joyce has definitely been there—and has seen to it that anyone else in the neighborhood can go, too—at a good rate and in convivial company. "I don't do Lubbock or College Station," she says. "The Fort Worth chapter used to have buses to College Station, but it was pretty confused and nobody ever took charge. I finally did it for about three years, but then I gave it up."

There have been a couple of memorable trips to Lubbock, where, sometimes, weather patterns appear that seem to have originated in another galaxy. "One time we went out there, and at kickoff it was a beautiful day: sunshine and 70 degrees," she says. "By the time we left the stadium there was rain, sleet, snow, hail, and a dust storm, and it was 28 degrees.

"We had another trip out there where, coming back, we hit a storm. The plane was going up and down, the wind was blowing, the flight attendants couldn't get up from their seats. It was horrible. It was the last plane out of Lubbock, and I thought we were going to die."

The most memorable trip, Joyce thinks, was one to Arkansas several years back. "We flew into Tulsa," she says, "and then headed to Fayetteville with a busload of people. As it turned out, that day the Longhorn team was late getting to the stadium, and nobody knew where they were. Once we got into Arkansas, about every 10 miles the state troopers stopped us and asked us if we were the Texas football team. It was hilarious. The team finally showed up about an hour before kickoff."

Among other memories, Joyce recalls a trip to Colorado, "where there was beer available at the stadium, and some of our students got a little bombed." She remembers Nebraska fans giving Ricky Williams a standing ovation ("Those people have real class"). She remembers Notre Dame, where, "the people were so nice and the tradition was just unbelievable."

Plus two Rose Bowls, one of them ending in a national championship. "I'm going to be high on that one for a long time," she says. "Really, it's been so much fun that there's no such thing as a bad trip.

"Unless we lose."

7

— J I M   W U C H E R —

'Hunnert'-Year-Old Hippie

It has been quite a number of years now since the world at large has heard anything from Jim Wucher.

"Most people don't know my real name," he says. "In fact, some of the people I run into on a fairly regular basis don't know me by any name at all." Wucher is comfortable with that. He dropped out of what is usually regarded as the "normal" world 30 years ago, and is not inclined to concern himself with small distractions. Big ones either, for that matter.

"My income now is … well, let's just say I'm on the edge of getting food stamps," he says, with a laugh. "I've got a Social Security check and a minimum state retirement check—a little less than $10,000 a year."

He drives a small pickup truck brightly painted burnt orange, with a white Longhorn logo on the door. Since 1983, he has held season tickets at Disch-Falk Field—home to one of college baseball's perennial powerhouses. When the Texas Longhorns journey to Omaha for the College World Series—which is most of the time—he is there, along with members of his adopted family, the Wild Bunch.

For the past 20 years or so, Wucher has been known simply as Hunnert—a nickname bestowed upon him by his friend Scott Wilson. It stands for "Hunnert-Year-Old Hippie" and has stuck to him like few things in life ever have.

Hunnert protests, mildly. Actually, he is only 77.

He doesn't remember exactly when he began regularly attending UT baseball games, but he found a scorecard from 1977 that he filled out ("I used to do that way back at the start"), so it has been at least since then. "Maybe," he says, "it was the national championship team in 1975 that got me started."

Since then, he has become perhaps the most visible presence at UT games, partly because of his distinctive appearance—long white hair drawn back in a pony tail, with a brightly-colored head band—and partly through his penchant for wandering the stadium rather than sitting in one spot. "Well," he says, "for one thing, my seat is in the middle of the row, and I disturb a lot of people if I get up to go to the john or go out to the parking lot to get a cigarette or a beer or a coke or a toke. But also, I just like to talk to people.

"We sit on the first-base side, but I like to go over and visit with people on the third-base side, or various people I know, or the cops, or the gate attendants, or the other standees. It's kind of a social gathering, and over the years I've become good friends with a lot of them."

It is probably a sure bet that most of them are unaware that—long ago—Wucher was a straight, upstanding, bona fide member of the proverbial rat race; a hard-working real estate salesman with a wife and four kids. Before that, he had also spent four years as an English major at Texas but left without a degree. "I've got 120 hours," he says, "It's just not the right 120."

In 1972, after 21 years of marriage, he got a divorce … and his life began spiraling off in a different direction. He got out of the real estate business and moved to Boston to sell pianos and organs—a business he had been in previously. It didn't work out, and within 17 months he was back in Austin, trying to figure a few things out. "I tried real estate again," he says, "but I had been gone long enough that I didn't know the market anymore, and I couldn't sell a damn thing … nothing. Then I wrecked my car.

"It happened one day after happy hour at a bar. I was headed home and hit a pole—missed a curve on 29th Street. It turned out that the car insurance I bought in Boston was only good for the calendar year. I bought it in April and it expired at the end of December. I had the wreck in January (1974), so now I basically had no job and was also afoot.

"So, rather than adjust my energies to maintain my lifestyle ... I adjusted my lifestyle to my income. I started cooking—went to work at a pizza place on Sixth Street."

At the time, the change was a radical departure from what Wucher had known for the first 45 years of his life. "I guess the real change came when I got divorced," he says, "but it didn't happen all at once. I went to Boston—I had friends up there—a married couple—that I lived with. I was actually doing well in sales, but the company did some things I didn't like, so I came back, and things just went from there.

"It was the same when I lost my faith ... it happened gradually, not suddenly. I grew up in the Baptist Church, and actually, when I was in high school and college, the neighborhood church was my social center. That's where my wife and I met. Once upon a time, I taught a lot of Sunday school classes there.

"From there, I went to a life of drinking beer, smoking dope, being a hippie, going to the joints, going to Willie's Picnic, the whole thing. Gradually, there were a whole lot of values I once had that didn't mean much to me anymore. I dropped out of a lot of things."

Wucher was born in Pittsburgh, and arrived in Austin at age 14, in 1942. "During the Depression, my dad had joined the reserves to bring in some extra money," he says, "So he was called up when the war started. We got mobilized and sent to Fort Polk, Louisiana, and then transferred here to Austin, where my mother stayed with the three kids while he left for the war. He went overseas somewhere but didn't see combat because he had been born in 1905.

"He came back after the war but he only stayed out about a year. He didn't like civilian life—he was used to being an officer, and having certain privileges. He was also a strict disciplinarian, and I was in his dog-house a lot—so I definitely grew up as an anti-disciplinarian.

"After I graduated from Austin High in '46, we spent a year up at Fort Dix. I was draft bait, so I enlisted for two years, because that way, the Army would pay for four years of college. I spent the two years at Fort Knox and then came down here to go to school at UT.

"I wasn't much of a sports fan back then, but I kind of got into it. I painted my boots orange and went to the football games carrying an ox bell. That was in the cowbell days."

Wucher also married, became a father, and nearly graduated. "I went to school for eight and a half long semesters and two summer semesters," he says, "but I never really had any goals or direction—I just had the GI Bill and was trying to do something with it. By the end of the fall semester in '52, I had a family and needed to get myself a real job."

His first job—investigating indigent claims for the state welfare department in Jacksonville, Texas—was, he says, "the worst job I ever had. I had that job 17 months. I bought a car, and when I got it paid off I quit and came back to Austin and got into sales."

Eventually, he wound up in Odessa, "because I had a brother-in-law there who said there was money to be made up there, and he was right. I went to work at an office job up there and nearly doubled what I had been making before. In fact, I got a raise when I interviewed for the job. They found out I was a stable family man with responsibilities, and that's what they were looking for. I did that job for two years, and also sang in a barbershop quartet. We were putting on a show one time, and a friend of mine over in Midland became impressed with me because I sold so much advertising for the show. He hired me to come over and sell pianos for him, and that's how I got into that business.

"I stayed in West Texas for five years and it was nice, but I finally got a chance to come back to Austin and I took it. I came through here once on my way to visit my folks, and they had opened up a new Baldwin [piano] store here, so I went in and got myself hired."

Although he came back to sell pianos and organs, Wucher was soon selling real estate. "I was trying to sell a piano one day to a real estate agent," he says. "I didn't sell him, but he liked my approach and hired me to sell real estate. I did well, but there was one time when I think I stressed 'em out a little bit: I sold a house to the first black couple to move into Northwest Hills, and I didn't tell my bosses about it because I was afraid they would kill the sale. As it turned out, the couple sold the house a year later. They were marooned up there in a sea of white folks and a long way from their day care, and didn't like it. But I sold real estate from then on, until the divorce."

Following the divorce, the sojourn in Boston (where he once again joined a barbershop quartet), the old world of Jim Wucher looked a little strange but 'Hunnert' has adjusted to it well. "Down there at the pizza place, we had a certain amount of walk-in business at lunch," he says, "but at night, it was basically a world of drunks, hookers, fringe people, dance halls, and shoeshine parlors, and I just kind of identified with that and the people in it. Blended in, so to speak.

"You didn't see regular people down there ... but that was before Sixth Street became gentrified."

As time passed, he expanded his repertoire. "I worked at a lot of places ... a barbeque joint, a chili parlor, a hamburger joint, and a full-service hotel. I also drove a truck on the state school campus for mentally impaired residents—delivering meals. The state watches the expenses on those people very closely ... kind of like the feds do on old people.

"I had one job where I didn't particularly like the music the young people who worked there were playing ... so I kept wet towels in my ears. That worked OK, except that during the lunch rush, when people wanted something, I couldn't hear them. So one day the manager called me in her office and started talking to me about softball, and how it's a game that requires teamwork, and how important that is. I thought she was talking to me about getting up a softball team at work. Turned out she was telling me I wasn't a team player, and I was fired.

"That was at 'Eats' out at Barton Springs. Then it became 'Good Eats.' Then it became extinct.

"I worked at General Sam's out on 2222, and I worked at a hotel on the river. They had a picture they would show you about how the food was supposed to be arranged on the plate."

He quit one job because his supervisor would not give him time off to go to Omaha with the Longhorns. "But the last job I had—for 10 years—was a part-time job with the state, so that was never a problem again," he says.

Getting to Omaha, in fact, has become something of an art form in Hunnert's case. "Since I started doing this," he says, "I've made every trip up there that the Longhorns have made—plus one that they didn't. That one was a little more laid back, since we didn't really care who won.

"I can always get a ride with someone. I'll share the cost of the gas and a hotel room—I can sleep on the floor if there aren't enough beds—and even if it turns out to be a 10-day trip, I can do it for $400. That's food, room, beer, and souvenirs. I know all of the ticket guys, so I hardly ever have to buy a ticket."

Once, when the couple providing Hunnert's ride arrived to pick him up, they found him with five pieces of luggage—of which four were cases of Lone Star beer. "It was for sharing on the way up," he says. "I didn't drink it all.

"I remember one time when we took 13 cases of Lone Star up there—not just for drinking but also for serving. We wanted to be able to serve those people a Texas beer if they wanted one."

The Lone Star ritual is part of the ever-evolving etiquette of Rosenblatt Stadium, wherein the fans of perennials such as Texas and LSU develop a bond and share tailgate areas. "Each year, it's like renewing old friendships," says Hunnert.

To muster up funds for these excursions, now that he is retired, he has developed a new sideline. "I'm into garage sales," he says. "Nowadays, everybody knows not to ask, 'Where'd you get that shirt?' They know where it came from: I can't afford regular store-bought stuff most of the time. Garage sales are also social events—there are regulars out there. In fact, sometimes regulars throw parties for other regulars.

"I also buy stuff for resale. I'll try to buy a piano or a canoe or a refrigerator—something that has to be hauled, so there's not as much competition for it. I've got a pickup and that gives me an advantage. In fact, I've done that so much that one time I arrived at a sale and some of the regulars were leaving, and they said, 'They don't have any canoes.'

"At the height of the season, there's almost a full page of them in the paper. The surrounding communities also have them, so I've been known to hit Dripping [Springs], Round Rock, Georgetown, Kyle, Hutto, Leander ... just about all of them."

Sometimes the trips bring interesting results. "I bought a canoe for $25 and then sold it to a couple for $55," he says, "and they were thrilled. They thought it was a steal. And I sold a piano for $550 that I paid $150 for. "Once I bought a canoe that leaked. I was going to try to fix it and sell it, and left it sitting in my front yard, and some kids stole it. So, you know, there goes my $15 investment ... but it's also kind of like putting a sack of crap in your yard and having someone steal it."

There are other occasional benefits, here and there. It helps Hunnert that his landlord has not raised his rent in 15 years.

As for the pickup truck ... "At one point," he says, "I started going with this middle-class lady, and I was driving an old, broken-down truck and I was pretty old and broken-down looking too, and I'm sure her neighbors figured she had picked up the yard man. But she talked me into getting a newer truck, and I got this one cheap from a garage where they had rebuilt the motor. The only problem was ... it was maroon. So she paid for the paint job."

Age, he figures, is a frame of mind. "I just got a checkup, and everything is pretty good," he says. "I'll admit to a touch of arthritis, a little high blood pressure, but it's not life-defining. Sometimes, my body or my mind does funny things: A few years ago, they threw a party for me in the parking lot at the stadium on a non-game day, and I missed it. I just forgot."

For minions of the regular world, dealing with Hunnert can often be a bit of a trial. "One time," he says, "I was driving Wilson's Cadillac and we were going through Oklahoma City, and I suddenly changed lanes real quick—at his request, because he said our turnoff was up ahead. The woman behind me did exactly the same thing—and got rear-ended by a semi. Nobody was hurt, but we all had to stay there and talk to the police."

The following exchange ensued:

Officer: "Do you have insurance?"

Hunnert: "Yes, I do."

Officer: "With who?"

Hunnert (pausing briefly): "I think his name is Bill."

Hunnert is gratified that, for the most part, his kids have accepted his change of life and accepted him into theirs. "My oldest daughter— she's married to an assistant DA in Odessa," he says. "She never forgave me quite like the others, but they have all done well with their lives, and I feel good about that.

"My oldest boy is retired from a job with the state, my youngest daughter has a good job in the computer business in Colorado, and my youngest son is very adept and has always done well in everything he has done. He goes to the ball games with me regularly.

"Last fall the oldest son and I spent a week up in Colorado painting my daughter's house and getting it ready for her to sell so she can come back to Austin. She's been there five years—she and her husband went up there with good jobs and bought a house, and within a year, he was dead of cancer. So she's looking to come home.

"As for me … I'm happy with it. I try to avoid regrets."

8

Rivalry

Not that it seems to have created any sort of deep-seated sense of insecurity, but during a long sweep of the historical record, it has been difficult for Texas fans to focus on one particular adversary and say, with clarity, "We hate those idiots worse than anyone else."

The field has often seemed a bit crowded, with three prime suspects emerging at various points: Texas A&M, Oklahoma, and Arkansas. Virtually all Longhorns have their favorites, but they are not always in agreement. The younger crowd will usually point at the Sooners, in view of the distressing recent events that were finally corrected only last year. Longhorns of longer lineage like the Aggies, who are, after all, the Aggies. Those who retain a fond regard for the old Southwest Conference are likely to pick the Hogs.

Suffice to say that for many years, with all three adversaries on the schedule, the Longhorns regarded their plate as full. At the end of World War II, a University of Oklahoma president is said to have declared, "We want to build a university the football team can be proud of," a reference to the school's determination to become a national power in an effort to erase bitter memories of the Depression and restore state pride.

Almost immediately, a spirited regional rivalry became one of the biggest games of the year nationally. The two teams battled in a packed house at the Cotton Bowl—an event preceded by an all-night bash in downtown Dallas. Over the last 60 years, many of these games have keyed a national championship for one, and a coaching change for the other.

And, for the almost exact 20 years that the careers of Darrell Royal and Frank Broyles ran a parallel course through the Southwest Conference, the teams annually engaged in Great Shootouts or other momentous battles.

Both of these rivalries, however, lacked one ingredient essential to the complete collegiate rivalry: proximity. The schools were simply too far apart to facilitate the kind of pranks and elaborate tricks that define the mature college relationship. Or as the pranks are often referred to in administration circles, "utter foolishness perpetrated by mindless degenerates."

Which brings us to the relationship between Texas and A&M ... each within easy striking distance from one another. In a sense, it can be said that the man who really fired up the rivalry was Charley Moran.

Moran went to College Station in 1909 to coach Texas A&M football, and it is said that he announced upon arrival: "I didn't come here to lose."

He was a man of his word.

The Aggies were quite successful under Moran, particularly at changing the character of a rivalry with the University of Texas, against which the lads from the farm school had a dismal record. It was Moran, legend has it, who spawned a permanent rivalry that was fought on the football field and through pranks and tricks both daring and idiotic.

Moran is the only Aggie coach who ever beat Texas twice in one year, and some decades later, just as the folks in Austin suspected, one of his stars admitted that, "from time to time, we used some boys of questionable academic pedigree." Moreover, the Longhorns complained, his teams took certain liberties with the concept of gentlemanly combat.

By the time UT angrily broke off relations with A&M after the 1911 game—in which the Longhorns were victorious but incensed over an injury to one of their players—Moran was roundly celebrated in verse over at the state capital:

"To hell, to hell with Charley Moran,
And all his dirty crew.
And if you don't like the words to this song,
Then to hell, to hell with you."

When the Southwest Conference was formed in December 1914, the two schools resumed relations, and A&M fired Moran in what most believed to be a concession to UT, in the interests of future harmony. Texas had not heard the last of Charley Moran, however. From exile, he wrote to Aggie players, urging them all to, "beat those people from Austin, if you still love me and think anything of me." The Aggies responded with a 13–0 upset victory in the 1915 game, in the first official year of SWC play.

Actually, the two schools had begun to take their athletic rivalry to heart even before Moran's appearance on the scene. In 1903, four Aggies were apprehended pilfering an Austin city limit sign and had the misfortune to be brought before a judge who was a UT graduate. A stiff fine followed.

The 1908 game ended with a brawl on the field, during which UT student William Trenekmann became the first known casualty of the rivalry, suffering a stab wound.

Also, by the time Moran left, the pregame bonfire had already become a tradition at A&M. It began in 1909 as a celebration of a victory over UT and eventually grew into a massive pyre over 100 feet high, built with 800-pound logs that made the *Guinness Book of World Records*.

In 1915, due to causes still unknown, the bonfire exploded. One witness recalled that it "scattered Aggies and bonfire from hell to breakfast and left a hole in the ground eight or 10 feet deep," But the Moran-inspired 1915 Aggie victory launched the rivalry's most famous episode.

In 1916, Texas avenged itself with a 21–7 victory, and the following year the school acquired a mascot—a cantankerous Longhorn steer peculiarly colored orange instead of brown, which UT intended to parade at the 1917 game with the score of the previous year's victory branded into its hide. Actually, the steer's debut was planned for the 2nd of March Annual Texas Independence Day celebration.

But the Aggies got wind of the plan, and one evening a commando crew piled into a Model-T Ford with branding irons and stealthily stole into Austin. The next day, the Texas mascot's handlers were appalled to discover their prize branded with the 13–0 score of the 1915 game.

The following day, an ad appeared in the Austin paper touting Bevo Beer—a near-beer that failed commercially but soon became the answer to the distraught Longhorns' dilemma. An enterprising soul in the UT camp took branding iron in hand, changed the 13 to a B, made an E out of the dash, and inserted a V before the zero.

At the 1917 game, the steer was paraded as "Bevo"—the name successive mascots have carried ever since. A brilliant recovery, although some may have wondered why a proud state university had named its mascot after an obscure beverage.

This was to be the first of four instances of steer-napping by the Aggies over the next 55 years. The original Bevo was not much of a success and was served at a joint Texas-A&M dinner a few years later. "It was pretty poor barbeque," one Aggie reported.

Ironically, Moran was destined to appear before the Aggies one last time—in an unusual role—and contribute to another great event in their history. Just as he had been responsible for the unplanned anointment of their biggest rival's mascot, Moran played a hand in the creation of one of the greatest of A&M legends—the saga of the Twelfth Man. The tradition stemmed from the events of January 1, 1922, when E. King Gill came out of the stands, donned a uniform, and stood at the ready if needed when the Aggies were short on troops due to injuries. The occasion was the Dixie Classic, a long-ago forerunner of the Cotton Bowl. The Aggies' opponents that day were the Prayin' Colonels from Centre College, coached by Moran.

The pranks between the schools cranked up again some years later. On one occasion, horrified Aggies were fed a rumor that the Longhorns had kidnapped and branded Reveille, the collie that has served as the A&M mascot since 1931. A group of panic-stricken Aggies rushed to the dog's pen, and found it asleep.

Many incidents revolved around the bonfires. Texas had its own for many years before discovering that the Aggies could be defeated regularly without it. Before the tradition disappeared, however, the Texas bonfire suffered an ignominious moment when a band of Aggies succeeded in lighting it on a Tuesday. With no alternative, UT students were forced to hold their bonfire ceremony two days before the game.

Meanwhile, each school continued to grow in the other's esteem. Longhorn contempt for the rustic Farmers grew out of early conditions, when A&M students lived in tents. For their part, the Aggies regarded Texas students as "tea sippers." The Aggies were once referred to in the Texas annual as a "pre-totemic society," and another Austin writer called their annual bonfire "a pagan ritual and fire dance."

In the early twenties, a pair of streaks began that would cause consternation on both campuses—for years, neither team could win on the opponent's field. There were a few ties, but no victories for the visiting team.

The Aggies' misery lasted longer. After a victory in 1922, they had to wait until 1956, when they threw an undefeated team at a Texas squad with only one victory to finally secure a win in Austin. Included among the Aggie failures was a 7–0 loss in 1940 that snapped a 19-game winning streak for A&M's defending national champions, and prevented them from going to the Rose Bowl.

The Longhorns' losing streak in College Station began after a victory in 1923 and was snapped in rather inventive fashion in 1941. That year, Texas students enlisted the helpful intervention of Madame Augusta Hipple, an Austin fortune teller. She told them to burn red candles.

Quickly, hundreds of red candles began burning all over campus, and the Longhorns smashed the losing streak with a decisive 23–0 victory. Thus was born a UT tradition that has gone through a change over the years.

Several times in the fifties, Texas resurrected the "Red Candle Hex" for key games against a variety of highly ranked opponents. Eventually, the hex returned to the status of being exclusively for the Aggies, and now the "Hex Rally" is an annual event before the A&M game.

In 1940, the series reached a period where Texas became so dominant that the Longhorns lost only three games to A&M over the next 35 years. Increasingly, the Aggies retaliated with pranks, raids, innovative redecorating, and anything else with which they could bolster their self-esteem.

Periodically, Aggies would fire the Texas cannon or hang a "Beat Tea U" banner on a Texas dorm. Once, they sneaked into Memorial Stadium and planted oats in a "Texas A&M" configuration. The oats sprang up at the first rain, much to the consternation of UT officials.

In retaliation, the Longhorns took to the air. In 1948, a UT student "borrowed" a plane and buzzed the Aggie bonfire five times. On each pass, he dropped a jug of gasoline with incendiary flares attached. One of them lit the bonfire, but the Aggies snuffed it out. On his return trip, the intrepid aviator ran out of fuel and had to put down in a field, where he used his remaining jar of gas to refuel and get back home. He was met by his dean and suspended.

The following year, two UT students loaded a car with explosives and sent it hurtling toward the Aggie bonfire. It missed, and they too were expelled.

In the early fifties, a UT grad flying a T-28 plane dive-bombed the bonfire. He overstressed the plane, which sheared the wings off, and crashed. He was killed instantly.

The next time a Longhorn ventured over the bonfire in a plane, the Aggies were ready. They shot it down. "Fortunately," a witness reported, "the police arrived in time to save the pilot from the mob, but they ripped the tail and wings off the plane and strapped them to the bonfire."

In 1949, an A&M student representative tried to defuse the situation by proclaiming that the hate between the two schools was "totally unfounded and more legend than actuality."

That year, Texas end Ray Stone was ejected from the game for decking A&M's all-conference running back, Bob Smith, with a right to the jaw, Aggie pranksters fared even worse. On the Sunday before the game, a carload of Aggies cruised up to the Texas bonfire and tried to ignite it. All that caught on fire was the back seat of their car, and two Aggies were hospitalized. Two days later, the survivors bribed a truck driver to help them, and he backed his truck up to the bonfire with a load of wood and three bombs hidden in the back. Again there was a miscalculation, and two more Aggies went to the hospital with burns.

In 1953, an 11-man A&M commando team slipped onto the UT campus, painted "Aggies" on a building and were happily applying a coat of maroon to some lawn furniture when they were caught by a crowd of Texas students. The Aggies were stripped, had their heads shaved, were painted orange, and then had to march at close-order drill before being thrown into a fountain. The Texas defenders were just getting back to sleep when a second group of Aggies showed up. They, too, were apprehended, and the whole procedure was repeated. When the Aggies were finally released, their car wouldn't start.

When Texas introduced "Smokey" the cannon in 1954, an "Aggie person" promptly kicked it over, causing it to fire a charge into the wall separating the stands from the field. No one was hurt. A few years later, the Aggies stole the cannon and sank it in Town Lake.

Meanwhile, glowing profiles of Aggie life continued to be published in Austin. "You may ask, who does go to Aggieland?" began an article in the Texas student magazine in 1960. "Not many, good sport, not many. Each year the enrollment drops, each year the Five Thousand Fanatical Farmers find it harder to keep out the women ('If the Corps wanted yew to have wimmen, they'd a-issued yew wimmen') and each year the poor Aggies sink deeper into a pool of nothingness, closer to extinction. One possible solution is to let females in: however, this would cause a number of problems. Can you imagine how warped a poor kid would be if both his father and his mother were Aggies?"

But in terms of off-the-field escapades, the Aggies more than held their own with Bevo's legions through the years. On the field, it was usually a different story. For more than three decades, Texas always seemed to have the talent, and the luck, to beat A&M. This was most graphically illustrated by events late in the day on November 28, 1963, in College Station. It had been less than a week since the assassination of President John F. Kennedy, and college football—like the rest of the nation—was in turmoil. Most of the previous weekend's games had been cancelled, but when Thanksgiving Day arrived, the Horns and Aggies squared off as scheduled.

It had not been a good year at A&M. Under new coach Hank Foldberg, the Aggies had only two wins and a tie to show for their efforts. Texas, on the other hand, stood at 9-0 and was ranked No. 1 in the nation. The Aggies were the last team with a shot at changing that.

They almost did. As the clock wound down toward the end, A&M was sitting on an improbable 13–9 lead. But the Longhorns proceeded to rise to the occasion, driving 80 yards for the winning touchdown on their last possession.

At one point, the Aggies thought they had stopped the drive with an interception, but the A&M defender who picked off the pass then inexplicably tried to lateral the ball to a teammate. The Longhorns knocked down the lateral, recovered the ball, and continued the drive.

Later, an A&M defender tipped a pass in the end zone, but was ruled out of bounds by the time he had possession. Texas then scored a touchdown, and won the game, 15–13. Slightly over a month later, the Longhorns crushed second-ranked Navy in the Cotton Bowl to affirm their national championship.

For the poor Farmers, it may have been the ultimate Aggie joke.

As the rivalry between the two schools continued, perhaps the most ambitious scheme emerged when the Aggies managed to steal every mascot in the Southwest Conference.

In his book, *We Are the Aggies,* John Adams writes, "Within a space of about eight hours one night, they set out in groups and stole every mascot in the SWC, including the Arkansas Razorback. The next day, when the state police arrived, they were all out there in a pen. The place looked like a zoo. The police questioned 700 students, and no one would give out any information."

The perpetrators were eventually identified—and soon had cause for concern, since one of the captives was Bevo. Stealing an owl or a frog was one thing. Stealing a steer, under the statutes of the day, constituted cattle rustling—punishable by hanging. After sweating in jail for several hours, they were eventually let off the hook, but another Aggie was less fortunate: he had lent the thieves his parents' Cadillac to go after the Baylor bear cubs. When they returned, the inside of the car was torn to shreds.

The last Bevo theft occurred in 1972, and the thieves had a flat tire on the way back to College Station, with Bevo in the back of a U-Haul truck. Presently, a state trooper showed up. The driver of the truck explained hastily that they were moving his grandmother's furniture. Suddenly, the 'furniture' hauled off and kicked the side of the truck, which began rolling back toward the patrol car.

"I see," said the trooper. "Well, you'd better be careful." Then he revealed an Aggie ring on his finger when he shook the driver's hand— and drove off.

Following this episode, the student councils of the two schools met, and conference-wide rules were set up prohibiting the pilfering of mascots and otherwise restricting pranks. Bevo began to sleep more easily at night. By that time, A&M had finally become coed, and the nature of the school began to change significantly.

For the Longhorns there were, of course, still Aggie jokes:

"The Aggies have purchased 300 septic tanks. As
soon as they learn how to drive them, they're going
to attack the University of Texas."

One individual who has a keen appreciation of this relationship is Mel Stekoll, owner of the famed "Cheerleader Car"—the orange '31 Chevy that delivered the cheerleaders to the sidelines at home games for 30 years. Stekoll has always held A&M in high esteem, as evidenced by the fact that he has probably committed to memory more Aggie jokes than anyone else on the planet. Among his favorites:

An Aggie goes in to see his doctor because he's feeling tired and run down. The doctor prescribes vitamins and minerals, tells him to run 10 miles a day, and check back in 10 days. After 10 days, the Aggie calls back and the doctor asks him if he's feeling better. "Well, not really," the Aggie says. "I still feel tired and run down, and now I'm 100 miles from home."

The Aggies, of course, have always returned this fond regard. Their standard method of revenge has been to take it out on the car.

"They stole it once," Stekoll says. "Stole it from right out in front of my house. What happened was, my son David was going to UT at the time, and he had also started a little business working on cars. He had two cars sitting in my garage that he was working on, so the Chevy was parked out in front of the house. I called David to see if he took it, and he hadn't. Then I checked the neighborhood to see if maybe some of the kids had rolled it down the hill. Then I finally called the police."

Stekoll soon had the car back, and is quick to register his disdain for the thieves. "Real quick," he says, "the police caught these two Aggies. They had hot-wired the car and were about halfway back to A&M when the police grabbed them. [They were] just driving down the main highway, in broad daylight, in an orange car with Longhorns painted on it. That shows you how smart Aggies are. It's about like if I had robbed a bank and then made my getaway in an orange '31 Chevy with plates that said 'Hook 'Em.'

"If they'd been smart—which of course Aggies aren't—they'd have put it in a truck or trailer or something. But I was fortunate to get it back—if they'd gotten it back to A&M, they probably would have put it on the bonfire. No telling."

The next time the Aggies struck, they didn't steal the car. They just modified it a little. "I came out there on the morning of the game," Stekoll says, "and my car was painted maroon ... and it wasn't wash-off paint, it was oil-based. The car was a mess. The Aggies ruined the side cover, and I sure couldn't take the cheerleaders into the stadium with that thing painted maroon.

"I ended up taking spray cans and painting orange over the maroon. It looked pretty tacky, but it was better than what they did to it." But then, Stekoll says, the Aggies are constantly making nuisances of themselves. "They've come over to UT several times and painted the fountain maroon," he says. "And Bevo's Bookstore up there on the drag next to the co-op—they sawed the horns off the steer out front four or five years in a row. I think they finally started stationing guards up there."

It hasn't all been one-sided, of course. Stekoll admits that several times, he tried to convince various worthies that with the proper planning, Reveille could be kidnapped. Finally, it happened. "I don't know, I may have had a hand in that," he says.

The event happened over the Christmas holidays in 1993, when the Aggies moved to Dallas to prepare for the 1994 Cotton Bowl game against Notre Dame. It involved extended surveillance by a group calling itself simply "The Rustlers." The dog they stole was a four-month-old puppy, which was in line to become the new Reveille. The group eventually staked out the Dallas residence where the pup was being kept, made the grab, and held the dog for several days.

The Aggies were in high turmoil: one school official called the theft a "serious felony," and unsuccessful attempts were made to get authorities to file charges. Finally, a tip was passed, and on New Year's Day the dog was recovered, unharmed, tied to a sign near Lake Travis.

In addition to that, Stekoll admits that for several years he was obsessed with a plan to strike the ultimate blow at A&M; the act with which he would achieve immortality. In the end, he came very close.

"For years," he says, "I had a thing in my mind to pre-set that Aggie bonfire. I mean, I thought about it and thought about it. I reached a point where I knew I had to figure out a way to do it. I always thought, 'Boy, if I can ignite that bonfire, it will be my claim to fame.'"

Finally, he went to see his son-in-law. "This was back in the nineties," he says, "and at that time my daughter, Tami, was married to a guy who was really into model airplanes and very smart about things like that. I asked him if it would be possible to build a model airplane that could be flown in there by remote control, with a bomb on it. He was kind of intrigued, but obviously, it was going to take some time, and a lot of planning.

"He spent a lot of time doing calculations and making drawings, and he finally figured out that we would need one with about a six-foot wingspan. I gave him some money, and he actually started building this plane. Of course, you never could get very close to that bonfire even at night, because they always had their freshmen out there guarding it. But he was building this plane, and we were actually going to fly it in there by remote control. He figured we would have to get within 200 yards, and we could send it in remote control from there."

But in 1999, something far worse happened at the Aggie bonfire. "He was actually in the process of building that plane when they had the tragedy at the bonfire," Stekoll said. "At that point, we scrapped the plan. It would have been the next year that we planned to try it."

Almost since its inception in 1909 (an alternate version has it that it began as a joke when an Aggie lit two trash bags), students from both schools seem to have been obsessed with the A&M bonfire. Long before Stekoll, a succession of UT commandoes launched regular attempts to either destroy it or light it prematurely, in the hope of sowing great anguish among the maroon legions. One was killed in the attempt.

As for the Aggies, with all their myriad traditions, they held few things as sacred as the pyre they simply but reverently called Bonfire. Aggies also died for the cause.

In 1955, an A&M student named James Edward Sarran was struck by a car and killed while guarding the bonfire. Sarran pushed a companion out of the car's path—saving his life—before being struck.

In 1981, Wiley Keith Jopling, riding on the back of a tractor during the building of the stack, fell off and was crushed under the wheel.

In perhaps one of the more notable examples of obsessive behavior, a Bryan police officer once tried to ignite the fire, failed, refused to explain himself, and was dismissed from the force.

As the years passed and the construction of the pyre became more elaborate, safety concerns increased. After the 1969 stack topped 100 feet, the administration took steps to curtail the height, but in later years injuries increased, and another student was killed in the nineties.

Finally, during a work shift in the early morning hours of preparation for the 1999 bonfire, the stack collapsed. When the debris was cleared, 12 Aggies were dead and dozens more had been taken to local hospitals. One of the greatest of all A&M traditions had become the scene of a numbing tragedy.

In the immediate aftermath, there was also a dramatic change in the relationship between the state's two largest universities. The longest, greatest, and most bitter rivalry in the great state of Texas was transformed into a massive demonstration of shared grief.

In the run-up to the game, Texas cancelled its annual Hex Rally, which was replaced by an evening vigil at the state capitol, attended by thousands of Aggies and Longhorns. Blood drives and relief funds were started, and officials from both schools made speeches and spoke of unity.

On Friday, Texas fans arriving in College Station for the game were greeted by A&M fans thanking them for their support. At halftime, UT's Showband of the Southwest played "Amazing Grace" and marched off, flying Aggie colors.

The Aggies upset the Longhorns, 20–16, and nobody got mad.

"At first, when that tragedy occurred, I thought they might actually cancel the game," Stekoll says. "But I think it helped soften the blow when our band paid tribute to them at halftime. A lot of Aggies even came over to our tailgates after the game and thanked us for being good sports.

"The war that went on … this sort of calmed things down. Now when we play, Aggies come over to our tailgate parties in Austin. Used to, you just didn't do that. There'd be a fight or something. They stayed in their area and we stayed in ours, and basically, we just didn't talk to them. But now, the rivalry has definitely cooled down because of that tragedy and the fact that we've been sympathetic to them."

While the Aggies had their bonfire, Texas has a unique victory totem: The Tower.

Originally known as the Main Building Tower, it was built in the early thirties, shortly after which Carl Eckhardt, head of the university's physical plant, got the idea of rigging it with lights to celebrate the school's achievements. With its size and prominent location, it was a natural landmark that, when lit up orange, could be seen for miles.

Eckhardt first lit the tower in 1937, and 10 years later began laying out what are now elaborate guidelines for lighting it. On various occasions it is partially lit, and sometimes is lit up totally orange, burning through the night.

Like the bonfire, it has been a scene of tragedy: August 1, 1966, when Charles Whitman climbed to the Observation Deck with a high-powered rifle and killed 16 people before being shot dead himself.

Known far and wide simply as the Texas Tower, it glows totally burnt orange after every football victory over A&M … and burns orange with a white "1" when the Longhorns win a national championship.

As for the Aggies …

"Things have kind of cooled off since the bonfire accident," says David Dunwoody, a member of the Silver Spurs. "That and the fact that everybody is kind of more sensitive to each other these days. But it'll be back someday. I've heard there's a steer out there somewhere with one horn … the Aggies thought it was Bevo, but it wasn't."

9

'31 Chevy Cheerleader Car

The way you have to figure this, it's got to be pure oversight ... something Mel Stekoll surely meant to do, at any moment, and just flat forgot.

Not that there is any quarrel with the esteemed family name: Stekoll is the descendant of Jewish immigrants from Latvia who came here more than 80 years ago, he says, "Because the Russians were after 'em."

Still, given the distinct hue that has attached itself to every other aspect of his life, you have to figure Stekoll always meant to have his last name changed to "Orange."

Just so it might be a more comfortable fit, you might say, with everything *else* about him.

Ever since the mid-sixties, Stekoll's persona—his very being—has been strongly associated with a unique car: a 1931 Chevrolet five-window coupe, painted orange and white, has become renowned in Texas Longhorn lore as "The Cheerleader Car."

Throughout most of this period, Stekoll also lived in an orange-and-white house in East Austin. For more than 30 years, he was the proud owner of a successful Austin business called "The Orange and White Paint Company." His wardrobe, like that of any loyal Longhorn fan, contains a large array of orange and white apparel, including sunshades.

Stekoll has even written up an entertaining little family history-style document that purports to conclusively demonstrate that the blood in his veins is, indeed, orange. Among his claims to verifiable Orangeblood status: the last time he missed a Texas-OU game was 1945.

When Stekoll and his wife, Martha, recently decided to move down to Lockhart, they looked at several different houses for sale. "The one we finally picked needed a little work," he says, "but the price was good and we were thinking about it. Then one day I was talking to the realtor on the phone, and he said something about 'the house on Orange Street.' "And I said, 'What? You mean the name of the street the house is on is Orange Street?' I think that's the one we want.

"So later we're standing down there in front of the house, and I told him we wanted to buy it, and his eyes kind of lit up, and then I told him that I would only buy it on one condition.

"So he said, 'Fine, what's that?' And I said, 'I need for you to go up and down the block ... on both sides of the street ... for about two blocks each way, and make sure there are no Aggies living in this neighborhood.'

"And he just looks at me with this stunned expression on his face, and he kind of started stuttering and stammering, and he finally says he can't do that because of discrimination issues.

"So I said, 'I don't discriminate against black people, I don't discriminate against Jews—I am one, I don't discriminate against Hispanics — I'm married to one, I don't discriminate against Arabians or anyone else. But I gotta draw the line with Aggies.'

"And his face sank, and he had this kind of desperate look in his eyes, and finally I couldn't keep a straight face any longer and I cracked up. I think he was very relieved when we signed the papers on the house."

The poor chap probably would have expected it, had he been better acquainted with Stekoll—to whom the Aggie joke is an art form.

Stekoll has an Aggie joke for every occasion. He has an Aggie joke when there is no occasion. He has Aggie jokes on his answering machine. He has a supply of condolence cards he carries in his wallet to hand people on any appropriate occasion—such as, if they happen to mention that there is an Aggie in their family.

In fact, in a recent book on Longhorns and Aggies, the author paid tribute to Stekoll as the man who told him the worst joke he had ever heard. "I think he kinda exaggerated that," Stekoll says, defensively.

Then again, perhaps it was some sort of Realtor's Revenge. Stekoll, who is "unfortunately, about to be 83," could probably be forgiven for thinking that his life has been jinxed since he moved from Austin. Since then, his house has been broken into, his car sabotaged, and he has had glaucoma surgery—which, he notes, is a little scary when you only have one eye to begin with (the other was shot out by an arrow when he was eight).

Worst of all, he and Martha have been obliged to maintain residences in two different cities so she can care for a niece who, for the moment at least, has been placed in her custody.

On the bright side, two old chums have been reunited: the car is back in action with a new motor.

And where Stekoll and the car are concerned—in terms of lifetime devotion, madcap adventure, and lasting fame (Longhorn style), no exaggeration is necessary. When the two first met, 47 years ago, it was not a pretty sight. The Chevy was sitting by the side of the road, broken down, forlorn and wearing a "For Sale" sign. "I found it down in New Braunfels," Stekoll says. "I was driving down the highway and saw it sitting over there to the side, with that sign on it. It was sitting out in front of a motor home.

"I'm only the second owner that car has ever had. I went in and talked to the guy—he had bought it brand new back in 1931 for $465. He kept it for years and then finally it quit running, so he gave it to his son, who was in high school. The son was going to turn it into a hot rod or something, but he never got around to getting it fixed. When I found it, it wouldn't start. So I bought it from the guy for $75. I've still got the original title that he had in '31. I pulled it back up to Austin behind a Jeep. Back in those days that's what I was driving—U.S. Army surplus jeeps.

"I found out pretty quickly why it wouldn't start—it had an old side-draft carburetor with leather gaskets, which were dried up. Every time you put gas in it, it just ran out the sides. So I got a new carburetor and fixed it up, and it ran for about another seven or eight years on the old motor. Finally, it broke down near Salado when we were going to the OU game —I drove it up to that game about 20 or 25 times over the years—and that's the first time I had to put a motor in it."

By that time, the Chevy had already become known as the "Cheerleader Car" and began to roll down the path toward fame and adventure. The road has not always been easy. Over the years, the car has been stolen, painted maroon, attacked by deranged Okies, and even sabotaged by one of Stekoll's relatives. However, it has always bounced back with sprightly gait, and a sunny disposition ... ever the faithful orange steed to the kindly gent who drug it out of the weeds nearly a half-century ago. Someday, when one them dies, the other will weep.

Stekoll and his car became permanently entwined with the Longhorn cheerleaders at a time when his own career as a UT student was long past.

"Unfortunately, I was born in Tulsa," he says, "but I've lived most of my life in Austin. I went to UT, but only for one year. My mother had a store over there on the drag that was real successful, but then her part-ner—who was also her sister—married a dentist from Fort Hood and moved to Columbus, Ohio. So I went to work in the store to do the bookkeeping. I only intended to stay there and help her for about a year, and then I was going back to UT. But I never made it back. I just stayed there working with her in the store until she finally sold it years later."

Eventually, life around the store became pretty lively. "There was a girl who came in the store a lot, and pretty soon I made a date with her," Stekoll says. "That was a no-no with my mother, but I dated the girl any-way. She was also one of the UT cheerleaders, and she fell in love with my car. I had it fixed up pretty well by then, and I had always supported the Longhorns and she was impressed with it.

"She ended up wanting to borrow the car ... [the cheerleaders] wanted to put speakers on it and drive it up and down the drag promoting the pep rallies. Back then they had a pep rally before every home game, which they don't do anymore. So we would go up and down the drag and they would talk through the speakers, and finally after a couple of years they decided to take it into the stadium. This would have been about 1965 or '66."

Thus was born "The Cheerleader Car."

"After that, at every home game, the cheerleaders rode into the stadium on the car," he says. "We did that for 30 years—until they took the track out in the nineties. After that we couldn't drive into the stadium anymore."

Over time, the nature of the operation changed a bit. "I drove the car for about five or six years," Stekoll says, "and then when my son David started going to UT, he drove it and I walked in front. That was because with the cheerleaders sitting on the front of the car, you really couldn't see where you were going very well, and somebody had to walk ahead and guide you. So that became my job. Also, when I first started, there were six cheerleaders. Now I think they have about 20. Pretty soon, just a few of them would sit on the car and the rest would go in front of it. It got to be quite a thing. I started taking it to other events, and I've been to a lot of parades. I've been in a lot of Cotton Bowl parades."

He has also taken it a few other places. "I've been to 60 Texas-OU games in a row now," he says, "and I used to take the car up there quite a bit—especially in the old days."

One of these trips became something of a mortifying experience for Stekoll, because those smart-aleck Okies discovered a painful fact about his origins. "One time, I took the car up there and had it parked out in front of the Hilton Hotel," he says. "Back then, there was this guy from Oklahoma named Sabatha. He was a full-blooded Cherokee and he had an old Model-T Ford—about a 1918 model or something—and it was all painted up like mine, except it was in red and had all OU stuff on it.

"He pulled a trailer behind it that said 'Boomer Sooner' on it, and he had a radio and TV and everything else in there. He also had his two front teeth removed and replaced with gold ones, and they had 'OU' implanted on them.

"That guy was crazier than me."

Presently, both cars were parked in front of the Hilton, and the usual crowd of reporters showed up to interview the two fanatics and check their driver's licenses. "In the course of this, unfortunately, someone asked me where I was from originally," Stekoll recalls, "and I said Tulsa."

He has since considered cutting off his tongue, but eventually learned to live with the consequences. "About 10 days later," he says, "I got a call from one of my cousins up there, and he said, 'Hey, did you know your picture was on the front page of the *Tulsa World*?' I said no, and he said there was a big headline over my picture that said, 'HE'S FROM WHERE?'"

Back in the day, the Friday night cruises up and down Commerce Street were even more entertaining. On one of those excursions, Stekoll and his pals found themselves confronted by Aggies. "One year," he says, "we were up there cruising Commerce, and we looked up, and right in front of us was a van full of Aggies. They had a horn in there that played the 'Aggie War Hymn' and they kept playing it over and over.

"My air horn was louder, so every time they turned theirs on, we drowned them out with 'Texas Fight.' Finally, about five or six of them piled out and came back to my car like they were going to attack us—but there were some police nearby, and they just herded them back into their vehicle, and we continued on.

"We never did figure out what a bunch of Aggies were doing at a Texas-OU game. But you know ... they do stupid things."

Another trip on Commerce almost turned out to be the last for Stekoll and the Chevy. "One time," he says, "me and a buddy of mine were cruising up there on Friday night, and we picked up this girl—a really good-looking girl—and she was sitting in between us in the front seat. There was really only enough room for two people, but she fit in real well. Then all of a sudden, about four or five Okie fans ran up and jumped onto the running boards and started rocking the car back and forth. It was kind of creaking and I was afraid something was going to bust, so I was trying to open the door.

"I reached through the window and shoved one of them, and he kind of fell over ... but then one of them jumped up on top of the car. The car, it wasn't really a hard top—it just had little wooden slats up there with a canvas cover over it. When the guy jumped on it, it just splintered, and then someone jumped on the front and the windshield broke. That's when I learned that the windshield was the original glass, not safety glass.

"The windshield just splintered and glass was flying, and one piece hit the girl and cut her arm open. They had first aid stations on every block—I think, basically, just to pick up the drunks that fell down—so we stopped at the next one. The cops came up and started chasing the Okies, but they just ran off into the crowd and [the police] never caught them.

"At the first aid station, they bandaged the girl up, but they said she needed to go to the emergency room and get stitches in it. So we took her to Baylor Hospital, which wasn't far away, and they stitched her up and we took her home. Wasn't exactly the best trip we ever made up there."

Stekoll got the car repaired, with safety glass, and life continued. As years passed, the car's fame grew quickly. "A lot of people used to think that the car belonged to UT," Stekoll says. "They would call the sports information department wanting to use it in some kind of promotion, and the people in the SID office would give them my phone number. At one time, it was featured on a postcard the school put out to promote the team. One half was a picture of the car and the cheerleaders and the other half was a photo of Smokey the Cannon, and then they had the season schedule on the back.

"There was a problem there ... the description on the car said it was a '31 Ford. I guess that is what they thought it was at UT. So pretty soon I got a call from an advertising manager at a Ford company saying they wanted to use my car in a commercial, and I just started laughing. And the guy says, 'What are you laughing at?' And I said, 'I don't think you really want to use a Chevrolet in a Ford commercial.'

"Of course, if you looked at the postcard, the Chevy emblem was very visible right between the cheerleaders, and it's really a very distinctive emblem. I wrote the company in Fort Worth that put out the cards and asked them to correct it if they made any more, but I never heard back from them."

Although the car was famous, it was not necessarily welcome just anywhere. "One time, I got this bug about seeing if I could get it into every stadium in the Southwest Conference," Stekoll says. "I got to where it seemed like something I really had to do. I got into every stadium—even A&M—except one. That year, when Texas got ready to go up and play Arkansas in Fayetteville, it was somehow decided that they couldn't take Bevo. I think they said the ride up there would be too much of a strain on him and they couldn't afford to fly him there, or whatever.

"Anyway, I saw my chance, and I talked to Al Lundstedt, who handled the equipment-related game passes. He said, 'We've got three passes: one for Bevo, one for the truck pulling the flag, and one for the cannon. You can have Bevo's pass.'

"So I drove up there. I spent the night about 50 miles away, because I knew I wouldn't be able to stay with that thing in Fayetteville. The next morning I drove to the stadium, hooked up with the cheerleaders, and went to see the stadium manager and showed him my pass.

He really was not inclined to be friendly. He looked at my pass, and he said, 'This pass isn't for your car. It's for that damn cow!'

"So I missed Arkansas, but I got into Kyle Field at A&M by driving [the car] in with the band. The guy on the gate just waved me through, although I think some of the Aggie higher-ups must have hyper-ventilated when they saw it, because security showed up and told me to park it by the scoreboard and leave it there."

One of the benefits connected with the car was that for years, Stekoll and his son David got into home games free. "We would just drive the cheerleaders in and then go sit behind the band," he says. "Consequently, we never bought season tickets for years—which we have to do now."

Consequently, they did have to buy tickets to road games, or resort to other devices. "I used to hang out with this guy who was a rodeo clown," Stekoll says, "and he would get in free to do his act and I would go in with him. One year at the OU game, David and I had tickets, but just for fun—I bet him I could get into the Cotton Bowl without using my ticket. Normally, that's a stadium where it's very hard to do that.

"But I got this big orange Texas flag, and when the band marched down the tunnel and into the stadium, I marched right in with them, waving that flag. Nobody stopped me."

However, boldly marching into what others would regard as absurd scenarios has always been a Stekoll specialty. As an underage enlistee in World War II, he was already being trained as a bombardier when the Air Force discovered that he had only one eye. "I got my right eye shot out when I was eight years old," he says. "We were living in a little town called Grove, right up in the northeast corner of Oklahoma where Arkansas and Missouri and Oklahoma meet.

"A bunch of us kids were shooting arrows at a target on a tree, and one of us would stand off to the side of the tree and pick up the arrows while the others would shoot. That's what I was doing—standing there collecting the arrows, when one of them somehow glanced off the tree and went right into my eye. They rushed me into an ambulance and drove me about 60 miles to Tulsa to the hospital, but of course, the eye was gone. There was nothing they could do.

"That's why, recently, I was sort of concerned when they told me I needed surgery for glaucoma. When you only have one eye, that's a little scary. But it all went well, and now the glaucoma is under control.

"Anyway, when the war started, I waited until I was 16 and then enlisted in the [Army] Air Force. You were actually supposed to be at least 17, but I lied about my age. They were trying to build up a force, and they were not that particular about it. I think if they felt you and you were warm, you qualified."

And the eye exam?

"The way I passed the eye test," he says, "was that they had you cover one eye and read with the other, and then vice versa. I read the chart fine with my left eye. Then when I was supposed to read it with my blind eye, I parted my fingers a crack, and read it again with my left eye. They never knew the difference. So I went through basic training for 90 days and was ready for advanced training. When you enlisted, they asked you if you wanted to train to be a pilot, a mechanic, or whatever.

"I don't know why I said 'bombardier,' … except that you heard a lot about that back then, and it just seemed the thing to do. So I started training. We were at Ellington Field, outside Houston and we were in a classroom for a while. Then in the second week, they took us out to this bomber for on-the-job-training. It had a Nordic bomb sight, which was very advanced at the time. So we went into the bomber and they started showing us how to work it.

"The proper procedure is to look through it with your right eye. Mine, of course, was artificial. So I used my left eye. They kept saying, 'No, no—use the right eye!' Finally, I had to explain to them that I couldn't see out of the right one.

"And they're going, 'What?' and they asked me, 'What are you doing in the Air Force?'

"And I said, 'Well, they gave me a physical but they didn't notice that I have a glass eye.' And they're going, 'What?'

"So I wound up spending 18 months in the Air Force, but not as a bombardier. They were all shook up because I passed their medical exam, but it really should have been obvious, if they had examined me closely."

Stekoll spent most of his adult life in Austin, working at his mother's store until she sold it, briefly selling real estate, then running his painting business for 30 years. He has been married three times and has three children. He and his third wife, Martha, have been married 36 years.

At that point, life began to get a little weird. "My brother-in-law—Martha's brother—has a few mental problems, along with an alcohol problem," Stekoll says. "He's been in and out of treatment facilities and his thought process is kind of unpredictable.

"He and his wife live in Harlingen and have a beautiful little girl, and two years ago Martha went down there for a visit and asked if she could bring her back up here for a visit, and they said fine. Two days later, my brother-in-law reported her missing, and I had a knock on the door and it was the police and the FBI.

"They checked on our niece and realized she was fine—and pretty soon they realized he wasn't, and they locked him up. When he got out, he threatened to kill me, and came up here waking the neighbors up in the middle of the night. Martha took the child to Chicago, where she has relatives, and I went to my sister's place for a while.

"While I was gone, he came up here to the house. He found some lacquer remover out on the porch, so he took it and poured it into the motor on the car. The next time I started it, it burned the engine up. So now, I have a big new motor in it. They had a hearing down there and Martha wound up with temporary custody of our niece because the judge ruled her parents were not fit at that time. But he also ruled that she has to live in Harlingen, so her parents can visit her. So now Martha is living down there in a house she already owned, taking care of her niece. The amazing thing is, she's just the brightest little girl you could imagine. But it's kind of hard on us."

It got a little harder on Stekoll recently when he returned home and discovered that uninvited guests had called. "They took everything that wasn't nailed to the floor," he says. "[They] got all my stereo equipment, and a lot of things that were valuable and irreplaceable. I had an old Edison phonograph from 1904 that my aunt in Tulsa left me years ago. It played cylinders and had a big horn on it. A guy that deals in antique radios and phonographs told me it was worth $4,000 to $5,000. So I've circulated pictures of it, but nothing has turned up.

"I also had some *Wizard of Oz* posters that, of course, can't be replaced. There was also a piece of sheet music—"Over the Rainbow"— that was signed by Judy Garland. In fact, she signed her name and then put "Dorothy" in parentheses, so I figure it was originally for a little kid.

"It really kills me to lose that stuff."

There is, of course, one saving grace …

"I don't think I could make it," Stekoll says, "if it wasn't for Aggie jokes. I just love Aggie jokes, and every time I get depressed, I think, 'Well, it could be worse, I could be an Aggie.'"

10

Rebirth of the Texas Cowboys

When the Texas Cowboys made their official re-entry into the campus life of the University of Texas in the spring of 2000, one of the main architects of their rebirth was Sam Bradshaw.

A UT service organization dedicated to promoting spirit and serving the university, the Cowboys had existed for 73 years, until they were banned from the campus in 1995 through an announcement from Dr. James Vick, then the vice president for student affairs. The action was taken following a perceived decline in the values of the organization over a period of years, culminating with the drowning death of one of its members, Gabriel Higgins, at a Cowboys picnic in April of '95. The banishment was for a period of five years.

At the time, Dr. Vick said, "It is our hope that when the Texas Cowboys return to campus, they will continue the tradition of service to the university and the community, and that they will redouble their commitment to the ideals upon which their organization was founded."

Among those who took that to heart was Bradshaw, a successful Dallas businessman and distinguished UT alum, who was deeply wounded by the fate of an organization that he had loved for 40 years. He spent five years on campus in the fifties, graduating in 1957 with a degree in engineering, served three years in the Air Force, embarked on a varied business career, and raised three children. Always he kept the Cowboys close to his heart. "The finest honor I ever had when I was in school," he says, "was being selected to be a member of that group."

To the outside world, the most visible aspect of the Cowboys is that they are the gents in chaps and Stetsons who fire the cannon—"Old Smokey"—at football games. However, Bradshaw and others regard that as simply one of the many functions of the group. "You had to be elected," he says. "The Cowboys were supposed to be the campus leaders, whether it was the captain of an athletic team or the student body president or what. That's what it was set up for, and somebody had to nominate you."

Off the top of his head, he can begin ticking off prominent members: Denton Cooley, Dolph Briscoe, Allan Shivers, Lloyd Bentsen, etc. "We were supposed to do service to the university and also perform good works out in the community," he says. "The motto says it all: 'Give the best you have to Texas; and the best will come back to you.'

"Over the years, so many of the people turned out by that organization have become the future leaders of society: politicians, corporate executives, doctors, lawyers, and scientists. We also always had our share of athletes, including people like Tommy Nobis and David McWilliams, but they were not all necessarily All-Americans. They were just good people and good citizens who upheld the values of the organization. In fact, I think there were seven Cowboys on the team when they won the national championship in '63."

One of the most significant roles of the Cowboys, Bradshaw says, is that for decades they served as the ambassadors of the university. "Once while I was in school there," Bradshaw recalls, "Adlai Stevenson came to give a speech. At the time, he was running for president against Dwight Eisenhower. And we were chosen to be his chaperones while he was on campus. It's just the kind of thing the Cowboys were expected to do."

Over the years, however, things changed. "I'm not really sure what happened," Bradshaw says. "I guess there may have been a period back there somewhere when school spirit just wasn't cool.

"It was always a very broad-based organization, with no single dominant group. We had Greeks, independents, athletes, people in student government; a really good representation of the whole campus. I think by the nineties it had become mostly Greek, and we lost the connection with the athletes—something we're trying to get back.

"It seemed by the mid-nineties that they weren't really doing any service for the university anymore … they were mostly just drinking and raising hell, and they were crossways with the administration over hazing issues and some other things. I know that by that time certain fraternities were filling membership quotas, and it just wasn't the same organization."

At a picnic in April 1995, Higgins—a "New Man" as new members are called—drowned in the Colorado River. His body was found to have an extremely high blood alcohol content and, following an investigation, the Cowboys' charter was pulled.

The road back began with the formation of the Texas Cowboy Alumni Association, and by 1998 a series of meetings was being held with university officials to determine what the makeup and character of the group would be when it returned to campus.

"Dr. Vick came to every meeting," Bradshaw says, "and Larry Faulkner, UT's new president, also played a big role. I know they were greatly concerned that when the Cowboys returned, it would be with the principles and dedication that we had once had, in the earlier years. It was very important to them that the Cowboys be reconstituted and reorganized in the right way."

In March 2000, at a reception organized by Bradshaw, about 100 prospective new members were introduced to an array of distinguished Cowboys from years past and given a strong sense of what the organization had stood for in the past—and would stand for again.

"One of the guys who spoke was [1974 All-American] Doug English, and I'll never forget it," Bradshaw says. "He looked at them and said, 'Men, we had it, we lost it, and we're going to get it back!' I think they were kind of awestruck."

Over the next three days the candidates were interviewed—each one by two Cowboys alumni and two members of the UT administration. From that emerged the first new class in five years with 41 new members. By that time, the alumni association had already established a scholarship in memory of Gabe Higgins.

"This will be our seventh year back," Bradshaw says, "and we've got the organization back where it should be. There are about 100 active members at a given moment, and we have a broad-based, campus-wide membership again. We've had two or three presidents of the student body, an editor of the *Daily Texan*, officers and members of student governing bodies and presidents or officers of fraternities and independent groups, members of the band, and athletes."

The Cowboys were formed in 1922 by Arno Nowotny, the head cheerleader, and Bill McGill, president of the Longhorn Band, in an effort to create a spirit squad that would support and promote UT athletics and perform other services to the university.

This group was to be formed from among the campus leaders, and the two chose 40 of UT's leading citizens for the job. It was announced in the *Daily Texan* that the group would perform stunts at the games and that the total cost of outfitting the Cowboys would be $500.

Nowotny, nicknamed "Shorty," was barely four feet tall, Bradshaw said. He remained at Texas for the rest of his life, becoming a popular dean of students. An award established in his honor is given each year to a student who exemplifies the traits of fairness, honesty, integrity, and unselfish service to the university.

"Back in the early days and I think up through World War II, new members used to be branded," Bradshaw says, "but they had cut that out by the time I joined. Thank God."

It was while Bradshaw was at UT that a precocious new member joined the group— "Smokey the Cannon", which made its debut in 1954.

As an engineering major, Bradshaw was soon on intimate terms with the new arrival. "I used to pull it around on a trailer," he says, "and they put me in charge of loading it. The original one wasn't very big. It would turn straight up and fired an aerial bomb. There was a little hole there where you could stick the charge in and then light the fuse.

"The first time we used it was at the A&M game, and although we won the game, it didn't work out too well. As soon as we got the fuse lit, some Aggie came by and kicked it over on its side, and when it went off the charge was fired straight into the stands. Fortunately, it hit the retaining wall instead of going into the stands, and no one was hurt, but it temporarily deafened the wife of the speaker of the House of Representatives.

"A few years later, the Aggies stole it and dumped it into Town Lake. Somebody eventually dug it out, but it was all rusted, and by that time they'd already gotten another one."

The Longhorns are now on their third one—Smokey III—and it differs slightly from the original. The current cannon and trailer are both authentic replicas of Civil War artillery and were handcrafted in Tennessee and Austin. The cannon stands six feet tall, is 10 feet long, and weighs more than 1,000 pounds. It has an electronic firing system and can fire five 10-gauge shells at once. The price tag is $15,000.

For Bradshaw, now 72, the rehabilitation of the Cowboys could be counted as his latest service to his beloved university: he served a highly successful stint as investment manager for the Ex-Students' Association and has served as president of various alumni groups.

"I was born in Troup, on the edge of the East Texas Oil Field," he says. "I graduated from Gaston High School [Joinerville] and came to Texas on a basketball scholarship. By the time I graduated [1957], I think I had about 160 hours, counting ROTC, and I went into the Air Force as a Lieutenant. I went in to fly, but they said they were going to hold me up, so I said, 'Hell with it, I'll do my three years and get out.'"

When he got out of the Air Force, Bradshaw went to work for Texas Instruments in Dallas and later moved to IBM. He eventually wound up doing securities and investment banking. In 1992, he formed his own company, Sam C. Bradshaw Investments.

Previously, in 1981, he and a group of investors formed American Cold Storage—acquiring public refrigerated warehouses, and he is now Chairman and CEO. "That one pays me a salary and I still do investments for a group of longtime clients," he says.

He and his second wife, Ruth Ann, have been married since 1978 and have three children. Lauren, the oldest, graduated from Washington & Lee and is an investment banker in New York. Amy got a communications degree at UT and is now an assistant press secretary for Sen. Kay Bailey Hutchison. Sam, the youngest, is still in school at Baylor. "This year," he says, "the five of us went to the Rose Bowl together. It was great."

Meanwhile, for a new generation of Cowboys, life on campus has returned to normal, and is getting better. "We add about 20 new members each fall, and bring in about 25 more in the spring," says Curt Wimberly, a senior accounting major from Kingwood. "On a continuing basis, we have about 100 members now. I guess it is about two-thirds Greek, but we have a lot of independents and a good representation campuswide.

"Membership is open, and the main qualifications are that you have to have at least a 2.5 grade point and you must have served in some kind of leadership role elsewhere before becoming a Cowboy. In my case, I was the treasurer for my fraternity when I was a sophomore. One of the standard requirements now is that at each interview, a representative of the university administration must be present." Of the total membership, four are elected each year to be the basic firing crew for the cannon, which was leased to the Silver Spurs for the five years of the suspension, but is once again manned by Cowboys.

Being on the firing crew is the most coveted role in the organization, but there are plenty of other things going on. "One of the things that is very important to us," Wimberly says, "is to regain the role of ambassadors for the university. We're taking steps in that direction.

"We are also involved in a lot of community service. We do a lot of work with the ARC of Austin, which is set up for the benefit of citizens with mental handicaps, and we're involved with Big Brothers and Sisters.

We also spend several hours a week at the Rosedale School, for severely handicapped children, where we run a Special Olympics.

"The basic requirement is that as a New Man you contribute 20 hours, and after that it's five hours. With other duties and carrying a full academic load, it can put stress on your schedule, but it's worth it."

There are also two concerts—Harvest Moon and the Spring Music Festival—where the organization has brought in top entertainers such as Merle Haggard, Jerry Jeff Walker, Dwight Yoakum, and Waylon Jennings. The concerts raise about $15,000 a year for ARC.

"I've had a lot of fun doing this," Wimberly says. "It's been an invaluable experience. It is, by far, the best thing I've done since I've been here."

11

Bleedin' Orange in Arkansas

By all of the usual yardsticks, Bill Edwards is a smiling, enthusiastic example of the normal Texas Longhorns fan. Constantly radiating an orange aura. Always prepared to support the cause. Never lacking the appropriate zeal. Fanatical, in fact.

He drives a white Lincoln with a personalized plate that reads, "Go UT." The car is covered with Longhorn stickers, and the horn blows "The Eyes of Texas."

Every day he wears a Texas T-shirt. It may be worn under a shirt if the weather's cold, but it's always there. Sometimes, he even wears orange shoes.

At home, there are UT flags displayed, and his room is full of Longhorn paraphernalia. One wall is adorned with a large oil painting of the Longhorn football team in a huddle.

Traditional roots? For several years now, Edwards, 60, has been back in his hometown, living in the house he was born in.

Actually, there is one small problem: If they ever hold a Dastardly Dude contest in Harrison, Arkansas, there will likely be only one name on the ballot. "I'm not very well-liked around here," Edwards admits. "I've been spit on, peed on, had beer poured on me, had things done to my car…I've had people scratch it up and down with their keys and I've had red paint thrown on it."

Some people have absolutely no sense of humor, and Edwards figures most of them live in Arkansas. Of course, residing in a community that sits an hour's drive from Razorback Stadium, his world view fits in about as comfortably as Bevo in a synchronized swimming event.

While his neighbors refer to Texas with a variety of inventive descriptions, to Edwards the Longhorns are "us." As in, "Every time they beat us

in anything, my phone rings all night with calls from people who say horrible things and then hang up. But when we win, they never say a word."

Edwards traces all this back to 1977, when he stepped off a plane in
Austin and fell in love. "I was 31 at the time and had been living in
California, working in the film industry," he says. "I grew up in Harrison,
but I had gone to UCLA to study film and got my undergraduate degree
there. I got hired right out of college and went to work as a writer at Disney,
and I spent about five years out there. I came home briefly, and then saw
where they were offering a Ph.D. program in film at UT.

"I applied and got in, and was also going to be a student teacher
because I also had a Master's degree. I went down there and just fell in
love with the place. It was still very reasonable [financially] to live there
then, so I decided to build a house. I went out and found a piece of land
way out in the country, in a place they were just starting to develop called
Cat Mountain. I built the first house there for $79,000. Today that house
is worth more than a quarter of a million."

Never much of a fan up to that point, Edwards discovered something
else: Longhorns. "We had such a great team in '77, I just kind of got
swept up in the whole thing," he says. "We were ranked No. 1, and that
tower was lit up orange, and I just got hooked. Notre Dame finally beat
us in the Cotton Bowl, but it was a great year. It was a whole new experience for me.

"I never was a Razorback. Well, maybe I was a fan as a kid just
because I lived there, but it wasn't a big thing. And although I was at
UCLA during the John Wooden era, for some reason I just never got
caught up in their sports programs. But Texas was different."His experience as a student teacher doubtless facilitated his conversion. "I saw that
they needed tutors in the athletic department," he says. "So I did that for
the next three years while I was getting my degree. I met all the players
and got to be friends with a lot of them.

"I knew a lot of the football and basketball guys, and they had all those terrific baseball players then—Calvin Shiraldi, Spike Owen, Roger Clemens—they all came to my house to get tutored, and we became friends."

Soon, a startling—some might say disturbing—transformation took place.

"I just got swept up in the Longhorn mania and became absolutely rabid," he says. "I was probably the most obnoxious fan Texas had. It got to where even Longhorn fans would tell me to shut up, because I just went wild at the games. But after tutoring them, all those guys had gotten to be like my kids. And I became a college football and basketball fanatic—I went to all the games. I went everywhere. I didn't care where it was."

However, Edwards was quickly provided with ample reason to revise that approach—in the case of one destination, at least. "I had become friends with some of the cheerleaders," he says, "and one night the basketball team was going over to College Station to play the Aggies, and the cheerleaders needed a ride over there. So I volunteered.

"They really had a better team than we did that year—I guess it was '78 or '79—but we won. Afterward, I took the cheerleaders to a pizza place near A&M so we could eat before going back to Austin. When we got ready to leave, there were Aggies all over the parking lot—tons of them. They had surrounded our vehicle with baseball bats—and they were beating the ground with the bats, screaming, 'You'll never get out of this county alive, you damn Tea Sips!' and doing their Aggie cheer and screaming at us.

"I thought we were going to be killed. There was only one male cheerleader, so it was me and him and the girls, who were all crying, and it was just awful. But the owner of the pizza place was a Baylor grad, and he called the police and they escorted us to the county line. It was the scariest night of my life.

"I'll never forget it, but I'll tell you what—it made me a bigger Longhorn fan than ever, because I saw what those Aggies are really like. So you can say I've had my life threatened for being a Longhorn."

Edwards stayed in Austin for six years, then spent the next 12 years in Dallas. "In 1983, I got a chance to go with a film company in Las Colinas, and that was my thing, so I went," he says. "Then when the economy went down I wound up working for American Airlines. Actually, I was in pretty good shape before I ever left California, and with the family business back home, I was doing this other stuff mostly because I wanted to."

In 1995, he went back home to see if he could be of help to his mother, Leota, running the family business. "We have a supermarket— Edwards Grocery—that we've had for 55 years in Harrison," he says. "I mean, it's a huge supermarket, with 36,000 feet of selling space. My father died when I was still in high school, and ever since then my mother has run it by herself.

"She's had an amazing run, but she's an amazing person. She's won a lot of awards: she was Grocery Woman of the Year in America, she was on the board of directors of Affiliated Foods in Little Rock, she's won all kinds of national "top grocery woman" awards. She is nationally known, and once received an award from President Clinton.

"These days, very few independent groceries are surviving anywhere, but we're still around. Wal-Mart tried to destroy us. They ran all theother supermarkets out of town, but we're still competing with them. My mother is 84 now, and this time last year she was still running the store. In fact, she won another award—Businesswoman of Arkansas.

"She's also had three bouts with cancer and beaten it … but the last one stressed her so bad she finally had a stroke. So now I'm just kind of helping take care of her."

Along with harassing the local rowdies that brandish their Hog Hats, it must be said that while Edwards may be the town's favorite target, he is hardly shy about dishing it back. "When they beat us down in Austin three years ago, it was the greatest thing in their lives," he says. "They're still writing about it in the paper. It finally reached the point where one of the newspapers asked their readers to sent in letters describing their favorite moment of all, in their years of following the Razorbacks.

"So I sent in a letter saying my favorite moment of following the Razorbacks was when Texas beat 'em for the national championship in '69, and they had to walk out of the stadium crying, with their heads down.

"I know. It was cruel of me to do that.

"After that, I had people come up and call me a son-of-a-bitch to my face and say, 'Why don't you get the hell out of Arkansas?' I would say, 'I'm a fifth-generation Arkansan, and my blood is *orange!*'

"Actually, an odd thing about that is that I was at that game—and I'm sure I was one of the few people who didn't really care who won. Back then I wasn't even a Longhorn fan. I just went because somebody gave me a ticket."

Edwards' battles with Razorback fans date back at least to the days of the Southwest Conference basketball tournament in Dallas. "I got into three fights with them down there," he says. "They were just always so rude. They would try to take over Reunion Arena and they called it 'Barnhill South,' and I would always get in their face and I would be saying, 'I know all about you people, so sit down and shut up.'"

When engaging in this sort of dialogue, it is a comfort to be 6 feet, 3 inches and 285 pounds. "I can back up what I say," Edwards says, but he notes that "once, the Dallas police came up and told me to shut up."

But, while acknowledging that he sometimes crosses the line himself, Edwards remains convinced that Arkansas fans are obsessed with Texas beyond the realm of rational explanation. "It's almost like a cult," he says. "They still write about Texas in the paper every day, and we haven't even been in the same conference for 15 years.

"The other night I was watching basketball on TV, and Arkansas was playing against somebody in the Southeastern Conference Tournament. The camera panned the stands and focused on the Arkansas fans, and one of them was holding up a sign that said, 'We Hate Texas.'

"The night that we got eliminated in the NCAA Tournament, people were calling my house saying, 'Texas is losing,' and they'd hang up. Arkansas wasn't even involved in that game. It all illustrates a point I've been making for years: they hate us more than they love themselves.

"Hardly a day goes by," he says, "that someone doesn't come up beside me in the car and give me the Hook 'em sign with the horns pointing down. Or some of 'em just drive by and shoot me the finger."

And Edwards, steadfast chap, never cracks.

"You know, my daddy always told me he didn't want me to go to the University of Arkansas," he says. "He said he wanted me to get a good education—and I did, at UCLA and Texas."

Besides, as far as the lineage thing is concerned, he figures the family has mixed blood.

"On my mother's side, they came from Texas long ago—from down around Glen Rose," he says. "I still have kin buried in a cemetery there. After that, my great grandmother packed 10 of them into a wagon pulled by an ox and came up here, where the rest of the family was.

"Anyway, I think that when my mother is gone from this earth, I will probably sell my part of the business to my brother and sister—and then I'll move back to Austin so I can be near the Longhorns."

12

Coaching Wheelchair Rugby

For James Gumbert, even at the distance of a quarter-century, it still seems as if he once walked into a nightmare and never came back. In the memory, the scene can still appear as horrifyingly surreal, and it—if reason prevails—will vanish with a snap of the fingers.

But it has never vanished. It is the life he has lived with since he was a high school senior in Waco.

The difference between then and now is Gumbert's attitude. "Life is what you make of it," he says.

It is remarkable what Gumbert, 42, has made of his situation in the years since a numbingly bizarre sequence of events long ago left him to face the rest of his life in a wheelchair.

In the beginning, there was the inevitable despair. But in the years since then, he has earned a college degree, had an extremely successful career in real estate, been married and divorced and remarried, and is now the head coach of two wheelchair rugby teams.

One, the Texas Stampede, is based in Austin, and the other is based in America—the U.S. Olympic Team. His world has expanded to include Athens, Greece, and Sydney, Australia, and various points in between.

Along with all this, he also became a Texas fanatic. Wherever the Longhorns go, there will likely be an orange-painted RV following them, with "Gumby"—as he is known to his companions—behind the wheel.

In fact, the only thing that bothers him about his peripatetic schedule with the rugby teams is that it sometimes interferes with Texas' football season.

But when the most recent one ended in glorious triumph in the Rose Bowl, Gumbert was there. And he is still whooping and yelling and celebrating. "Dude," he says, "if you think I'm going to shut up about something as great as this, you're crazy."

It has been a long journey since the moment he realized that one life was over ... and that he would have to build another. It began on Christmas 1980. "I grew up in Waco, and it was my senior year in high school," he says. "I was pretty much your basic high school kid. I played football and baseball—that's what you do in Texas—but golf was really my game. Back then, my ultimate dream was to be on the PGA Tour one day."

But fate intruded.

"On Christmas night, I had a one-car accident," he says. "The car rolled over, and I wasn't wearing a seat belt. I broke my neck.

"It didn't seem that serious at first—I walked away from the wreck and they put me in an ambulance and took me to the hospital, where I had surgery.

"Then I walked out of the hospital on January 1, with no medical or neurological problems. I was wearing a neck brace and was under doctor's care, but I was free to resume my life and get on with my senior year. I went to class, played golf, did everything normally except that I was wearing the neck brace.

"In fact, things were really going well. I had been around golf all my life, and I had worked at a golf course since I was eight or nine. That spring, I was winning tournaments and played myself into a college scholarship."

Then Gumbert went for a checkup, and learned that there was a problem. "They discovered that a bone that was in my neck that had been grafted from my hip had not healed the way they wanted," he says. "At that age, your body is still growing, and the graft had not taken in the way they would have hoped. They basically said, 'It's your choice: live the rest of your life with the neck brace, or let us do more surgery and go in and fix it.'

"At that age, I had no frame of reference for that, and they were basically saying 'Let us go in and do it differently and it will be better.' So I agreed. After all, I hadn't even missed any school with the injury, and I didn't figure there would be a problem."

The date has remained fixed, forever, in his memory. "It was Easter break, spring break, whatever," he says. "I walked into the hospital on April 13, 1982, and they did the surgery. And something went wrong.

"The long and short of it is … due to complications, I died on the operating table. They had to revive me. Later, when I came to in the hospital bed, I didn't feel bad. Basically, I didn't feel anything. Then they told me I had died as a result of the surgery itself, and they had to bring me back.

"And I said, 'OK … why am I having trouble breathing?'

"And they said, 'You're paralyzed.'

"And I said, 'Oh, God …'"

Looking back on his life today, Gumbert says, "One thing you will never hear me say is, 'I wish.'"

Gumbert's attitude and his personality are unfailingly positive. He has turned a permanent disability into a personal statement: a life of achievement and fun out of a shattering blow. He gained satisfaction from what he can do rather than living in anguish over what he cannot.

But it was a long road.

"The attitude I have about it today did not come easy," he says. "You have to remember, I'm 24, 25 years into this now. It's different in the beginning—for everybody. When I walked into that hospital, I was a guy who had a golf scholarship to college, still had the world at my fingertips, living the American dream.

"When I woke up in the hospital bed, I had to face the reality that that life was gone, forever. All those physical things I had done every day up to then—I couldn't do anymore. You have to ask yourself who you are now.

"There is the 'Why me?' part of it, and I certainly experienced that. Some people get stuck in it forever. I've had people say to me, 'I don't see how you deal with it.' The thing is: how do you *not* deal with it? It's your life, from now on. The choice is to spend your life at home, or go out and build another life.

"You get really frustrated when people say they know how you feel, because they don't have a clue. But one day, I was sitting there with this halo device around my neck, and some guy came in and was by my bed and talking to me, and I couldn't see him because I couldn't turn my head. He was saying, 'I know how you feel,' and I got angry and told him to get out. Then out of the corner of my eye I caught a glimpse of him as he wheeled himself out the door, and it dawned on me, 'He does know how I feel.'

"We talked a lot after that, and it was a great help to me. I still talk to that guy today.

"As far as the 'Why me' feeling goes ... you finally have to realize that these things happen, for whatever reason.

"Every day, somewhere, somebody has an appointment with the worst doctor in the world."

Gumbert decided that the best way out of his grief was to help others get rid of theirs.

In 1988 he got a B.S. from the University of Texas Health Science Center in Dallas and began working for the Texas Rehabilitation Commission, "trying to help others in this situation basically get from point A to point B and then get on with their lives. I felt that it was something I could do with my life that would be useful and helpful to others."

Then he got a call from an old buddy that turned into something big.

"We had been best friends in high school," Gumbert says, "and he called me about a property that had come open out where he lived by a golf course. I told him I didn't want it, but it might be a great place for my parents to live. We got together with them and bought the property and they moved in. Then he called me about another property out there, and we bought it and sold it, and made some money on it.

"And then he said, 'Why don't we get into the real estate business?' and I said, 'Because we don't know anything about it.' So he said that if I would go to school and get a real estate license, he would do the leg work and I could be the brains of the operation. So we did that, and pretty soon we had our own little real estate company in Waco.

"By this time we had both gotten married, and the wives got involved in the business, and we started buying houses and flipping them, and eventually got into property management. We did that for four years, without really knowing what we were doing, and made a lot of money. It worked out very well for both of us.

"We finally sold the company in '92 and divided the assets, and went our separate ways, and we were quite pleased with ourselves."

But around this time, his first marriage ended in divorce. "She was a girl I had grown up with—we had known each other practically from the cradle," he says. "She had two kids from a previous marriage, and I got into the dad thing pretty well, but it may be that we just knew each other too well.

"We made it four years and then went our separate ways. She's a great lady and I still talk to her a lot, but it just didn't work out."

It was at this time that Gumbert moved to Austin and became involved in wheelchair rugby.

"I was in good enough shape financially, from the real estate, that I could do pretty much what I wanted," he says, "and what I wanted to do was become a wheelchair rugby player.

"What [the sport] is ... is full-contact rugby played in wheelchairs on a basketball court. It's like these Mad Max chairs running into each other up and down the court." A documentary film on the sport, he notes, is titled *Murderball*.

For Gumbert, after years of being treated as an invalid, it was as if a fresh gust of wind had blown into his life. "It pretty much changed my life," he says. "It changed the way I saw myself, and the way others saw me. That excited me.

"It brought back something from my youth that I had missed ... something I hadn't seen in so long."

After years as a player, Gumbert switched to coaching a few years ago. Wheelchair rugby is now played in 22 countries and entered the Olympics as a demonstration sport in '96 and a medal sport in 2000.

Throughout this time, Gumbert was also a Longhorn fan—a situation that ratcheted itself up to another level when he bought an RV and became acquainted with the ladies and gentlemen of the Rolling Horns.

"For a long time," he says, "there were a bunch of us who used to tailgate on the roof of a parking garage over between San Jacinto and Trinity, and it grew to the point that we started taking a van over there, and finally, an RV just seemed like the next step.

"So one day I told them I was going to buy one, and everybody was like, 'What—how are you going to drive it?' And I said, 'I don't know.' But I found one on eBay, a 34-foot 1996 Winnebago for $31,000, and I bought it three years ago. Now I've knocked out a back wall and put a lift on it for the chair, and I can even drive it."

Therein began a series of often-comical adventures involving a determined band of neophytes in the RV world that included Gumbert, his trusty sidekick, Curt, and eventually his future bride, Kelly Mae.

"I bought it a week before the OU game, and that became our first trip," Gumbert says. "Just me and my buddy, and two guys in chairs. We built a ramp to get the chairs in—that was before the lift—and drove up to Dallas. We didn't have any clue where to park. We didn't even know how to dump the tanks. We didn't know anything except we had us an RV and we were tailgating.

"We didn't even have any regalia on it to show who we were. But we got up to the Cotton Bowl, and we met these people—real friendly—who said, 'Hey, you gotta park in here with us,' and this one guy guides us in and shows us where to park.

"So we get out, and the guy who helped us looks us over and says, 'Son of a bitch—they're Longhorns!'

"So there we were, on our first outing—parked at the Texas-OU game with a bunch of Okies. But they turned out to be really nice people, and the guy who helped us park has since become a close friend. He even comes down to Austin for some of our rugby games."

Somewhat later, the entourage embarked on a more ambitious journey—all the way to the Holiday Bowl. "That was another deal where we just took off without knowing much about what we were doing," Gumbert says. "If anything had gone wrong we would have been SOL. We still didn't know anything about RV etiquette. We didn't know there *was* etiquette. We'd pull into a restaurant somewhere and take six parking spaces, like we were J. R. Ewing or something.

"We didn't know a good RV park from a bad RV park. We had tickets to the game but no idea where we would park. Frankly, when we got to California, we really looked a whole lot like the Beverly Hillbillies. When we got to San Diego, we just lucked out and drove straight to the right spot."

Smack in the middle of the Rolling Horns.

"That was a group we'd been looking for but could never locate at the stadiums," Gumbert says. "We knew there were a bunch of Longhorn fans who drove RVs to the games and tailgated together and we wanted to meet them. This time, my buddy comes back into the RV and says 'They're parked right next to us.'"

And so, the Hillbillies joined the Horns. A perfect fit.

"You couldn't find a more open, accepting group," Gumbert says. "We've met all these great people that we've been traveling with ever since, and it's like a family. It's really an incredible soap opera … we're all involved in each other's lives. Any time you find people who believe what you believe and love what you love, it's hard to let go."

The next item was the wedding, and by this time, Gumbert's RV was properly decked out in orange. So was everything else.

Describing his bride, Gumbert says, "Kelly is just dynamite … she's really changed my life. So few of us get that second chance in life, to meet someone dedicated to doing anything they can for you." In other words, a fine woman who became a Longhorn in self-defense.

The original plan, following a church wedding, was to have the reception at a local establishment—which burned down a month before the wedding.

"So we had the reception in the UT Alumni Center," Gumbert says. "She had picked out some kind of cinnamon dresses for the bridesmaids, which showed up burnt orange in the lights. They played 'Texas Fight' and the 'Eyes of Texas' and finally Kelly said, 'I give up.' Her family is originally from Chicago, and she had to learn to appreciate the Longhorns. But she's as orange-blooded as the rest of us now."

Presumably, she realized she was marrying a man who has, in his front yard, a 350-pound cement Longhorn, four feet long, three and a half feet high, and painted orange.

Gumbert is awaiting comment from the neighborhood association, but he isn't that worried about it.

"Like I said, life is what you make of it," he says. "To me, mine has been full of so many wonderful people, it's been an incredible experience.

"Don't ever feel sorry for me. I've been blessed."

13

Walkin' Away from A&M

Occasionally, as one travels down the long road of life, there may be certain endeavors that seem to draw parallels elsewhere. In that regard, the legacy of being a true, orange-blooded Texas Longhorn might be compared to the acquisition of wealth—some are born to it. For others, it requires a little effort.

Which brings us, of course, to Jay Parmelee.

Now 58, Parmelee is a successful Dallas realtor with a wife, two teenage daughters, two degrees from UT, and all the aspects of the "good life," Longhorn-style. He has attended back-to-back Rose Bowls, and in his time has watched Texas win two national championships in football and several in baseball. He contributes to the Longhorn Foundation, and has established himself as a staunch, loyal—perhaps even renowned— UT fan.

But it was not always so.

In the spring of 1965, when Parmelee was a senior at Rockdale High School, his immediate future seemed preordained. Prepackaged even. Stamped and labeled. Signed and sealed.

If, at the time, someone had suggested to the assembled minions at Forty Acres that young Jay would soon be joining them, Bevo would have keeled over in shock.

The matter of Parmelee's collegiate experience had seemed almost settled from birth. The family's ties to Texas A&M were solid, and it must have seemed that when the sun rose and set each day, it had a distinct maroon tint to it. There seemed no doubt that he would soon become another proud Aggie, and everyone involved was very comfortable with that thought. Everyone, that is, except the intended victim.

"I was raised on a ranch," Parmelee says. "My dad was a veterinarian by education ... he had graduated at the top of his class at A&M. He had just always envisioned me as going there too. He had gone there when he came back from World War II. He was already married by then and he went to A&M and got his degree in veterinary medicine.

"I wasn't actually born in College Station, but my mom always told me that's where I learned to walk. We lived there when I was a little kid, and I got to know the campus like the back of my hand. The guy who lived next door to us was the band director. He's the guy who wrote 'Spirit of Aggieland.'"

When John Parmelee graduated from A&M, he and his wife, Mary, moved their growing family to Rockdale and bought a ranch. But not much changed except the location. "From then on, my dad was a rancher," Parmelee says. "He never actually had a veterinary practice, but he always said that what he had learned was useful to him every single day, working with the livestock on the ranch.

"My mom always thought that I had A&M ingrained in me. After we moved to Rockdale, we still went over to College Station for the football games, and all of my Future Farmers of America activities in high school were centered on A&M."

Parmelee played football and baseball in high school—he retains vivid memories of a death-defying act: trying to tackle Bellville's Ted Koy and landing in the hospital, but the only scholarship offer came from Baylor, which didn't interest him.

By that time, however, the first signs of aberrant personal behavior had surfaced.

"My dad and I talked about it throughout my senior year," he says. "At first, I told him I wanted to go to SMU. And he said, 'Well, I'm certainly not going to pay for that.'

"Then I started talking to him about TCU, and the point I used to try and talk him into that was that they had a ranch management program there, and I told him I wanted to get into that.

"But he countered that by saying, 'Well, if you want to come back to the ranch afterward, why wouldn't you go to A&M and get the best agricultural education possible?'"

So, what was it that SMU and TCU had that A&M didn't? Practically everything.

They were located in large cities with an upbeat, urban culture and no mandatory military requirement. Most of all, they had large numbers of female students.

Texas A&M today, with 40,000 undergraduate students, a huge infrastructure, a first-rate curriculum, an urban environment and dozens of entertainment venues, is one of America's most diverse and rewarding educational options. The dreaded Corps of Cadets—though still a centerpiece—involves only a small percentage of the campus population. And there are now thousands of married couples who met each other as students there.

But that is not a description of A&M during the first six or seven decades of the Twentieth Century. At that time, it was a relatively small, all-male, military-agricultural school located, as the usual description went, "in the middle of nowhere."

In those days, being an Aggie required a great deal of dedication. Fanaticism, one might even say. And Parmelee was not interested in becoming a fanatic.

With SMU and TCU sidelined, he tried again.

"Texas had come up in the conversation as sort of an alternative," he says. "Austin was about the same distance away as College Station, and I had already seen enough of it to know it would be a great place to go to school.

"Once in high school, when we were in the playoffs, some of us were hurt, and our trainer took us over to UT to be treated by Frank Medina.

Later, when I was going to school there, every time Frank saw me he just called me 'Rockdale.'

"Anyway, we were there long enough for me to get kind of excited about it and take in some of the flavor of the place—particularly the women.

"So, to convince my dad to give his consent for me to go to Texas, I said I had decided to go to law school."

Once again, ol' dad sidestepped the thrust. "We had a distant relative who was one of the assistant professors at the UT law school," Parmelee says. "One day, dad and I drove over to see him. I was really excited. My dad never did anything without a purpose, and I thought then I had it made. Here we were going over to talk to one of the profs at the law school, and I figured the reason had to be that he had actually decided I was right about going to Texas.

"Well, we got over there, and the guy proceeds to tell me that the top three grads from the law school the previous year had done their undergraduate work at A&M, and there was no reason why I couldn't go to A&M and get the benefit of the discipline and all, and then come over to law school at UT. That was why my dad wanted me to talk to him.

"I was crestfallen ... I don't think I said a word the whole way back home."

At this point, a decision was made to take the bull-headed kid by the horns, so to speak. "I had never actually filled out an application to A&M," Parmelee says, "and by now it was getting pretty late in the summer. So shortly after the trip to Austin, Mom and Dad and I drove over to A&M. Because I had never actually applied, I basically had to take the SAT over there. While I was doing that, Mom and Dad were getting me enrolled.

"This was in '65, when the Corps was still mandatory, at least for freshmen, I guess. I went to orientation, and then I spent one night there. The next day, I was scheduled to go do some more orientation stuff. Part of that was getting my head shaved.

"By this time my parents had left, thinking I was there to stay.

"I left, too."

By all accounts, it was a clean getaway.

"Basically," he says, "I hitchhiked my way down to the coast ... I just kind of hung out on the beach for a week, thinking things over. My family had no idea where I was. Finally I came back. By this time, high school had started and they were opening the football season. I knew where they were playing, and I ended up back over there at the game.

"My mother was there with my sister. My dad wasn't there. So I sat with my mother and sister and rode back home with them. Pretty soon, I talked to a friend of mine who was at A&M, and he told me I had been reported AWOL.

"At home, we sat down and talked all through that weekend. I told them I just did not think A&M was the place for me.

"Finally my dad said, 'Well, you walked away from A&M, so if you think you're man enough, you just make your own decision, and I won't stand in your way.'

"One of the things here was ... all those years I had worked on the ranch, I had cattle that I had raised and sold, and every time I did, my dad took the money and put it in my college fund. So by this time, I had earned enough money to pay for my college. I think that figured into my dad's decision. Frankly, I figured I had earned the money, and that gave me a right to have a say in where I went, and he conceded that."

And so, Parmelee was soon on the road again, with his mother. "We got packed up and drove down the farm-to-market road down to the main highway," he says. "When you got to the highway, if you turned left to the north, it took you to Austin. If you turned right, to the south, that led you to College Station.

"When we got to the highway, my mother stopped and said, 'Which way are we going?' I just kind of gave her the 'Hook 'em' sign and pointed to the north, and that's the way we went.

"Before we left, my dad gave me a hug and said, 'Whatever decision you make, I know it will be the right one, and I'll stand by it.' And that's what he did till the day he died."

For Parmelee, who eventually got two degrees from UT—a BBA in 1970 and an MBA in '71—there has never been a regret. "I knew from the moment I hit the campus in Austin that I'd done the right thing," he says. "I've never had a second thought."

His father, eventually, also became comfortable with the thought. "One year, when we were getting ready to play A&M over in College Station, the [Silver] Spurs were really concerned that Bevo was going to be kidnapped," he says. "They were looking for a place to hide him out, so I volunteered our place ... without telling my dad.

"You should have seen the look on his face when he drove up and saw Bevo's big old trailer sitting there on our property. We had some barns and pens up near where the house was, and Bevo was in there. My dad took it all in great spirits. Bevo stayed there a couple of nights, and then the Spurs came and got him and took him to College Station for the game."

Parmelee, who walked on for one year in baseball, says he was at Texas, "at a great time," which included a national championship in football achieved with the famous 1969 victory over Arkansas in Fayetteville, followed by a Cotton Bowl win over Notre Dame. Although he has recently followed the Longhorns to two Rose Bowls, he says he watched the '69 Arkansas game on the tube.

"I didn't go up there in '69, because I had gone up there in '67," he says. "After that experience, I swore a blood oath that even if I knew it was the last football game I would ever see in my life, I would never go to another game in Fayetteville. If you were driving with Texas plates up there, you couldn't buy gas, you couldn't stop and go into a place and eat ... once you were in Arkansas, about the only thing you could do was get a hamburger at a Dairy Queen. Even in Oklahoma, if you went up through Tulsa, you could buy gas and eat. But once you crossed the line into Arkansas, you were out of luck. So I watched that game on TV."

Through the years, Parmelee—whose big sport as a kid was baseball—has been a frequent presence at UT baseball games. He has had season tickets at Disch-Falk Field for 25 years and has made numerous trips to Omaha for the College World Series, in addition to various other locales.

"At one point, we had a home-and-home series with Arizona State that ran for several years, so every other year I went to Tempe," he says. "There were some years where they basically had a major league franchise waiting to happen, and one time I was out there when Barry Bonds was playing for them as a freshman. He was sure a lot leaner and lankier then than he is now."

His fondest memory, perhaps, is of the time he and a buddy were invited to sit in the TV booth at Rosenblatt Stadium during the college world series. That year, the Longhorns had a deep pitching staff led by All-America lefthander Greg Swindell, a future major leaguer—and notable prankster.

"The way the bracket was arranged then," Parmelee says, "is that if you won your first three games, you then played a basically meaningless game before going into the finals, and that's what was going on. We were playing Oklahoma State and getting hammered like 18–13, using our backup pitchers.

"I was just having fun up there in the booth. Jim Fregosi was up there doing color, and I was sitting there listening to the ESPN feed. Suddenly, they got all excited because they spotted Swindell down in the bullpen.

"What he was actually doing there was standing behind the catcher, whose back was to the field, guarding against stray line drives. And he was wearing a right-handed fielder's glove. Pretty soon, just fooling around, he started throwing the ball right-handed. ESPN picked up on that, and they went nuts. They thought they had the scoop of the century—Greg Swindell is coming in and pitch right-handed in relief.

"They were jabbering about it, and pretty soon Fregosi had had enough and he started calling them stupid SOBs and telling them how ridiculous they were, and I'm thinking, 'Well, I hope that mike isn't open.'

"But by that time it had spread, and all these people just went flying down there en masse. One guy was running down there with this big camera and fell down. It was hilarious—Greg was just leading them on."

Parmelee and his Longhorn baseball pals—who frequently included members of the "Wild Bunch", such as Austin attorney Scott Wilson—truly distinguished themselves on a road trip to Miami a few years later.

"It was the year they had all the Haitian riots down there," Parmelee recalls. "The Longhorns were playing a weekend series, and on Friday I kind of manufactured a business excuse and flew down there. Scott was with the attorney general's office at that time, but he had gotten off and was already down there and had a room I could stay in, so I flew into the airport and rented a convertible.

"When I got there, all the people from Haiti were rioting downtown. I drove over to the hotel and picked up Scott and Jose Peña (another Wild Bunch member), and we went to the game that night. After the game, we drove back and found a place to eat ... and all during this time there were sirens going off and police cars going around everywhere, and you could see the smoke coming up from the area where the riots were.

"After we ate ... well, we had all had more than one or two pops by then ... we decided to go down and check out the riots—something to tell the grandkids about and all. So, we go down there, but we really didn't get anywhere close. I mean, it was literally a wall-to-wall traffic jam. So like about half the rest of Miami we're sitting there in this gridlock and we're going nowhere.

"Finally, I decide to get out of the car and walk up ahead and see what's going on. By this time, Wilson has already struck up a conversation with some homeless person sitting there on the curb. Between Scott and Jose, you've got two people there who never met a stranger.

"I left them there and started walking, and when I got a couple of blocks down the street, I ran into some barricades and this guy was saying, 'You all have to stay here because they don't want anyone past this line.'

"So I started mouthing off, and pretty soon this cop grabs me by the arm and says if I try to go any further he's going to have me arrested. And I said, 'What the hell do I care? I've got the attorney general of Texas back there in my car, and I'll be out of jail before you finish the paperwork.'

"And he looks at me and says, 'You brought your own lawyer?'

"So he marches me back to the car … and there's Scott, sprawled out in the front seat, passed out. And there's Jose, sprawled out in the back seat, passed out.

"And the guy looks at Scott and then looks at me and says, 'This is the attorney general of Texas?'

"I just kind of shrugged. I didn't have much of a comeback for that."

Eventually, Parmelee's life more or less hit a normal groove.

He got into the real estate business immediately after graduating at UT, and later got married and began raising a family. He never went back to the ranch, as far as earning a living was concerned.

He has been with Lincoln Properties in Dallas for 12 years, and is now vice-president. He and Carol, his wife, have been married 20 years and have two daughters—Brennan, 15, and Courtney, 13. His dad died 10 years ago, and his mom now lives in Houston.

"I don't go to as many games as I used to," Parmelee says, "but I still make quite a few."

There is also an ironic connection to a time long ago. "My best friend from high school is now a retired coach, and he lives in College Station," he says. "We always go to the UT-A&M game with him whenever it's played in College Station, and we really enjoy it. He lives about two blocks from that house where my parents lived long ago."

Reflecting on the path his life has taken, Parmelee says, "If you compare A&M today to A&M back in 1965, it's like night and day.

"But I'm a Longhorn. I've been a Longhorn for 40 years, and it's been nothing but good times."

14

The Silver Spurs

It is sad to report, but it seems a rift may be developing between two of the University of Texas' most revered traditional icons.

We refer, of course, to Smokey and Bevo.

One is a handsomely made cannon, which erupts loudly at football games every time the Longhorns take the field or score. The other is a splendid fellow, quite robust, but with sensitive eardrums.

"The cannon gets to be a problem every year at the OU game in Dallas," says David Dunwoody, one of the four members of the Silver Spurs who served as handlers for the Texas mascot during the 2005 season.

"It's because of the close confines of the stadium sidelines there," Dunwoody says. "There's not much room, and every year during the game we're about 15 or 20 feet away from the tip of that cannon. Every time it goes off, so does he."

"He" meaning nearly 2,000 pounds of startled Longhorn.

"Every time that thing goes off, you'd better hold on," Dunwoody says. "Wrap that rope around your hand—even though you're not supposed to. It could be a choice between getting your hand torn up or getting some kids stomped to death."

There does seem to be a partial antidote, however—if the Longhorns can score often enough. "After about six shots of that cannon, he finally just gets tired of fighting it and calms down," Dunwoody says.

And in Smokey's defense, it should be noted that young Bevo—he's only four years old at the moment—tends to react similarly to any loud commotion or unfamiliar movement in his immediate vicinity. In time, he may adjust.

Through the years, for the long succession of Texas mascots and their handlers from the Silver Spurs, it has always been a matter of adjustment.

A petroleum engineering major from Houston, Dunwoody was one of four seniors—along with Garrett Godwin of Kaufman, George Wommack of Midland, and Ross Sutherland of Uvalde—selected as Bevo's handlers for the memorable national championship season.

"The Silver Spurs is an organization that typically you join as a second-semester sophomore or first-semester junior," he says. "You get put up by the guys in your fraternity, and you fill out an application and go through an interview process.

"Each candidate is interviewed by the older members to find out what your character is, what your interests are, and how you think you can be of help to the organization. Each semester, somewhere between about 18 and 24 new members will be selected. The total number of Silver Spurs at a given time will vary between the high 60s and low 90s, depending on the size of the classes.

"Every year, in February or March, four new handlers are chosen for the next year. They are virtually always seniors, because they have to be people who have been in the organization long enough to understand its purpose and to become fully involved in it. They also have to be four guys who have had the time to spend time out at the ranch, and spend some time around Bevo."

Clearly, the desired objective here is to be one of the handlers. So, what do the other 65 to 85 members do? "Have a good time," Dunwoody says, laughing. "But we also raise money. We're associated with Neighborhood Longhorns—which is local schools in Austin. We do a lot of charity work, and we give $10,000 a year to the schools to use at their discretion. We also give another $8,000 to $10,000 in scholarships to UT students, and that amount is about to be raised.

"There's also now a Bevo XIII Endowment, and in the future that's what we'll run off of. At the moment we still run off fund-raising from members. It's a privately funded organization, so we're not officially controlled by the university."

The name Bevo XIII refers to the most recent retiree, one of the most remarkable mascots in UT history. The current successor, Bevo XIV, is also beginning to look like a remarkable chap.

Traditionally, the mascots—all longhorn steers—have come from a variety of sources. The very first one was said to have been picked from down on the Mexican border, and there have been many donors over the years. But there have been only two Bevos over the last 20 years or so, and they both came from the same ranch.

"Bevo XIII is 22 now, and he was the mascot for 17 years," Dunwoody says. "I think that may have been the longest tenure for any one mascot, and he came from the ranch belonging to Betty and John T. Baker. They've gotten real close to the Silver Spurs, and they've been just great to us.

"When it came time to select a new mascot, they had a steer out there that looked very promising, and he's the one that was eventually picked. So the Bakers have provided the last two Bevos."

Bevo XIV has one readily distinguishing characteristic—he's a lot bigger than anything around him. "I don't know for sure, but he may be the biggest mascot UT has ever had," Dunwoody says. "I know he's bigger than the last one, and he's a lot bigger than any other steer his age. You can look at photos of him with the other steers his age, and he just dwarfs them all."

At his inauguration, however, this was not readily apparent. "The switch was made at the opening home game in 2004," Dunwoody says. "There was a big ceremony, and they brought both of them out onto the field. Right before the kickoff they officially retired XIII and introduced XIV, but he was just a little kid at the time, sort of wandering around out there like, 'What's going on?' He had these little stubby horns, and everybody was going, 'What's he doing out there?'"

Slightly over a year later, they were looking at a different animal.

Last checked after the Rose Bowl (he turned four in April of '06), Bevo XIV was turning into quite a sight. "The span between the tips of his horns is now at 60 inches," Dunwoody says, "and he weighs about 1,750 pounds. He's six feet tall at the shoulders, and he's about three to four inches taller than the other animals his age … and he eats about three percent of his body weight each day."

The feed comes in several forms—two kinds of hay and a molasses grain feed, but fortunately, feeding him on a daily basis is not part of the handlers' job. "During the school year he's kept out at the ranch—about 45 minutes from Austin—and the owners feed him," Dunwoody says. "He gets the grain in the mornings and evenings and eats the hay as he pleases."

And, if you check the driver's license closely, his name ain't really Bevo. That, of course is a revered and regal title—something like "Your Majesty"—worn by all Texas mascots.

"His real name is Sunrise Studley," Dunwoody says. "We call him Stud."

Blending a gent of this description in with four student handlers to produce the desired effect at football games, public appearances, benefits and parties is, indeed, a matter of adjustment—on both sides.

"He's actually a very docile animal," Dunwoody says. "He really doesn't want to hurt anybody."

That, however, doesn't cover the half of it. "The starting responsibility of our job is to get him harnessed and get him to the event on time," Dunwoody says. "And that isn't always easy. The first thing is to get the halter on him … and sometimes, he just doesn't feel like going anywhere. He can be very ornery.

"Basically what we have to do then is just chase him around until he gets tired, and then throw it on him. You basically kind of throw it around his horns, and he finally realizes he's caught and just stands still, and you can put it on his head."

For both Bevo and the Spurs, this is preceded by a process of getting acquainted.

"If he doesn't know you very well—and he's not used to your mannerisms and your being around him—he's not as likely to let you put a halter on him," Dunwoody says. "Once he's used to you, you can kind of come up inside his horns—you have to move real slow and be ready to move real quick—and put your arm on the inside of his horns so that he can't get you.

"So if he turns, the horn doesn't hook you, and you can get in there and put the halter on. He's kind of gotten to where at that point he knows he's going to have to wear it … so he'll just put his head out there for you to put it on. Then you just cinch it up and go."

Hey, what could be simpler?

"In the beginning," Dunwoody says, "we weren't real sure how to get in there and he'd turn before you could get in there close enough, and he'd catch you in the face, or the shoulder, or whatever."

One would suppose the horns are capped …

"Not really," Dunwoody says. "In fact, if you look closely, it almost looks as if they've been sharpened. Actually, nothing's been done to them at all."

Hanging around Bevo on game day can definitely sharpen one's sense of survival. In a stadium filled with 60,000 people, minding a large animal that hates any kind of commotion around him can be very exciting.

"When we were up at Baylor," Dunwoody says, "we're up against the end zone, and there were no students there—but they run all their damn students through that tunnel—so all of a sudden they come storming through that tunnel, screaming and yelling, and we've got him standing there, and any kind of commotion like that just freaks him out. If he doesn't have a barrier around him protecting him from these people, he just wants to take off, so that's what he did.

"So here they come, running through there acting crazy, and then some kid sets off a foghorn … [Bevo] just took off running straight at some photographers, and we're just hanging on, skiing down the concrete, just jerking the ropes trying to stop him. Finally he stopped. I think he just saw a lot of people in front of him, like a barricade—otherwise, he would have been gone."

This incident could be a helpful primer on the accepted technique for corralling a stampeding longhorn. "You just hang on until he stops," Dunwoody says. "You can try all sorts of things to try to make him stop, but it's not going to happen. He's definitely done that to us a few times. When he feels surrounded, he just kind of acts from instinct and defends himself. At DKR (Memorial Stadium), he's real docile and he's got a lot of room to kind of walk around and hang out, but occasionally he'll get bothered by a noise or something.

"A couple of times when we were trying to turn him around, he's charged two or three of us and stuck his horn right in someone's back. Each time we've been lucky enough where we kind of caught him. He's already acting weird, so you're keeping an eye on him … already moving away from him.

"He just lifts up as soon as you move away, he's taken my shirt up, and he's taken Garrett Godwin in the leg. You just constantly have to be aware of how far away from him you are … and get a feel for his demeanor, and always be ready to throw your forearm up, because you'd rather have him hit you there than in your back or the side of your head."

Having the occasional horn run up your back definitely sets off the game-day experience, Dunwoody says. "For the rest of the game, every time the wind blows, your shirt basically blows off," he says, laughing. "It's definitely a different experience.

"Sometimes some serious things happen. There have been a couple of times where guys got hit in the back and it actually punctured. There was a guy a few years ago who was hooked in the nose—the horn actually came up and ripped through the nose.

"I think it's just a matter of being aware; you can sense his anxiety, and he recognizes his strength and that he can overpower you. But he's never gored anyone—it's more like a slice than a stab. Like any other animal, he just gets scared sometimes. Or, you may get hit when he's just trying to swat a fly on his back. But he's not trying to hurt you."

Sometimes, mishaps can even occur during the Bevo selection process. "When they were trying to decide which animal to use for the new Bevo," Dunwoody says, "they took another steer out to a party to test him, and they were shooting pictures and he just took off. He nearly ran over a little kid—someone yanked [the kid] out of the way—and drug his handlers through some cactus."

But for Dunwoody and the Silver Spurs, life with Bevo has afforded far more highs than lows, and one of the biggest came in the OU game, when the Longhorns emphatically smashed a five-year losing streak. "Those Oklahoma people have done a lot of trash-talking the past few years when they were winning," he says, "but I think they expected us to beat 'em this year. We almost got into a couple of fights last year, but I think this year they were waiting to get spanked.

"They have a group up there called the Ruffnecks, and they drive that Sooner Schooner around the field. We have a running bet with them that each year the president of the winning team's organization gets to shave the heads of the president of the losing team's organization.

"So I've got pictures from this year of their president getting a *T* shaved into his head at the 50-yard line, and it's really great."

"Looking back, I would have to say that my whole career at UT is something that was just meant to be. All my friends are here. I've done well with my grades. I just had a chance and ran with it. It was a lot of hard work and a hell of a lot of fun.

"I really enjoyed going to all those football games with Bevo. It's just really neat to be associated with something that everyone just flips out over. Little kids … their eyes just get so big when he comes in.

"Everybody just drools over Bevo."

RIGHT:
Ken Capps with
Bevo at his annual
OU Weekend party.

Courtesy of Ken Capps

LEFT:
Radar Thomas
(aka J. M. Thomas, Jr.)
with unidentified
companion.

Courtesy of Radar and Lila Thomas

LONGHORNS FOR LIFE

RIGHT:
Radar Thomas
standing in front
of his house.

Courtesy of Radar and Lila Thomas

LEFT:
Bevo relaxing at the ranch between games.
Courtesy of Mel Stekoll

RIGHT:
Ken Capps with Bevo and two members of the Silver Spurs in Austin, circa 1973.
Courtesy of Ken Capps

LEFT:
Silver Spurs Garrett Godwin (left) and David Dunwoody (back to camera), licking their wounds after a tussle with Bevo.
Courtesy of David M. Dunwoody Jr.

RIGHT:
Silver Spurs (l-r) George Wommack, Garrett Godwin, David Dunwoody, and Ross Sutherland with Bevo in front of the Texas Tower.

Courtesy of David M. Dunwoody Jr.

LEFT:
Jim Wucher, alias "Hunnert," leaning on Mel Stekoll's car.

Courtesy of Mel Stekoll

ABOVE:
Mel Stekoll's big moment: getting into the Texas-OU game without a ticket by marching into the Cotton Bowl with the band.

Courtesy of Mel Stekoll

LEFT:
The Cheerleader Car in front of Littlefield Fountain.

Courtesy of Mel Stekoll

LEFT:

Ken Capps at the moment the clock ran down to zero at the Rose Bowl.

Courtesy of Ken Capps

RIGHT:

Adam Blum (left) and Frank Denius at the Rose Bowl.

Courtesy of Marvin E. Blum

LEFT:

Ken Capps, wife Laura, and son Adam with the Texas Tower in the background, lit up orange with a "1" for the national championship.

Courtesy of Ken Capps

15

The Rolling Horns

Out there in the great American mainstream, they would probably mark Bill Trigg down as being a little strange.

For one thing, he has a burnt orange dog that has a rather singular view of the world.

Then there is his finesse with women. How many guys do you know who won a girl's heart with a speech about corny dogs?

There is also that crowd he hangs out with—a fun-loving highway armada calling itself the "Rolling Horns," that has given new meaning to the phrase "following the team."

We also have his tender advice to his kids: If you want ol' Dad there, don't get married during football season.

Speaking of which, when he and Rose, his fianceé, scheduled their May 27 wedding, they selected a small, tastefully appointed chapel just off I-35 in central Austin. It's called Darrell K. Royal-Texas Memorial Stadium.

"Actually, we did check the UT sports schedule to make sure that wasn't the week of the College World Series," Trigg says. "It was upstairs in the club room. The men were outfitted in black tuxes with burnt orange ties and cummerbunds, and the ladies wore crème and burnt orange."

All of this coming from a guy who got his college degree from the University of Houston. "When I was a kid, Darrell Royal was my idol. In fact, one of the first books I ever read was about him, called *Doing It My Way*."

"Also, when I was a kid, it was a tradition every Thanksgiving that the family watched the Texas–Texas A&M game on TV at my grandmother's house. Some in my family were Aggies, but most were Longhorns. It just kind of got to be a tradition: I always felt that if I was from the state of Texas I should be a Longhorn, because that was the state university."

Although Trigg was a multisport star in high school, no scholarship offers came and, he says, "at the time our family finances were not such that I could go off to school in Austin. So I went to work full time and went one full year at UH, and then did eight more years of night school till I finally got a degree in business. Back then I worked for ADA Oil Company, which was a Phillips 66 distributor owned by Bud Adams.

"I also worked in the Oilers office, where I ran their in-office printing press. Back in the days before Kinko's and outlets like that, companies did their own printing. I had to give up on having the regular college atmosphere, but I got what I needed. I went into business for myself, and I've been doing that ever since."

The business is Gulftex, and it is still in Houston, although Trigg moved to Austin about 10 years ago. "We manufacture and install metal walkway canopies for schools and churches," he says. "We do business all over the state, but mostly in the southern part. I go over there and tend to things about two days a week now, but I live in Austin."

Through the years, the success of the business allowed Trigg and his first wife, Judy, to concentrate much of their efforts on raising kids and going to football games. "She died of a stroke two years ago," he says. "We have four kids, and now I have seven grandchildren. Rose has two children from her first marriage, so it's a pretty big group."

As the years passed and Trigg's fascination with the Longhorns grew into—dare we say fanaticism?—one thing became abundantly clear to him: as a total experience, professional football was no match for the college variety. "Back when the Oilers were in Houston, Judy and I were big fans," Trigg says. "We had season tickets for years and went to all the games, but a pro game is just that—a game. You go to the stadium, watch the game, and then leave, and that's it.

"College football is so much more than just the game: it's the entire atmosphere—the band, the cheering section, the stadium, the campus, the students, everything. The first football game my father ever took me to was at Rice Stadium, and I saw the Longhorn band and Big Bertha, the drum, and I was enthralled.

"Another thing I like about college football is [that] your favorite player isn't going to be traded to another team. Sometimes they sign early with the NFL, but that's easier to adjust to.

"The thing is, you get to meet them and be around them at a time in their lives when they're just kids, and they act like kids and think like kids a lot of the time, and it's fun to feed off that energy and enthusiasm. They still have a passion for it, before it becomes just a business."

Trigg also eventually realized that if one seizes the opportunity, tailgating can become a lifestyle. This, in turn, leads to the exotic world of the RV. "Judy and I used to make regular trips with the Flying Longhorns," he says. "We went to San Francisco when we went out and played Stanford and New York when we played Rutgers, and it was fun.

"Then about nine years ago we got connected with some people who had an RV, and we tailgated with them some. Pretty soon we started renting RVs a couple of times a year—maybe OU and A&M—and did that for about six years, and finally I just went ahead and bought my own."

For Trigg, this opened up a world of fun, adventure, new friends, new experiences, and new relationships. At Longhorn games and elsewhere, RV areas are like clumps of small towns. Friends park together ... for years.

"I've had people say to me, 'Doesn't it just ruin your good time if your team doesn't win?'" he says. "And I say, 'You've got to understand something: what we do from August to, hopefully, on into January, is tailgate season. We just use the Longhorn football games to determine the location of the next tailgate party—so everybody knows where to show up.

"It is an incomparable feeling if we win the game—that just makes it better. But it doesn't destroy your weekend if we lose. Not if you're a fan and you love your team, because we'll be there next week, wherever the team is."

However, while being fun, the lifestyle of the nomadic tailgate enthusiast also comes with the odd dire warning or two. "For home games," he says, "we all typically show up on Thursday afternoon. You have to do that to make sure you can park where you want. We tailgate, and we watch the football game, and finally go home.

"We're there until mid-day on Sunday. You're going to spend four days to go to a three-hour football game, but that's what it's all about. If you're going to do this, you'd better not have a 9-to-5 job; you'd better have a position somewhere that allows you to do this. If you're working a regular job, you'll lose it.

"Also, if you're going to spend the money for a motor home, you do it because you plan to use it. They're not economical. Let's face it, they're not a cheap way to travel. If you're worried about the cost of the fuel, don't buy one."

The type that Trigg drives, he says, gets about 6.5 miles to the gallon and sells for, "about $185,000 on up.

"If I hadn't done this, I could have stayed in a lot of expensive hotels all those years," he says, laughing. "But I would have missed a lot."

Including Rose.

"We met last year during OU Weekend—October 8—on the State Fair grounds," he says. "We met, of all places, at the Fletcher's Corn Dog Stand after the OU game."

Ah, yes—one of Dallas' legendary rendezvous points, for sure.

"There were about 30 people in our tailgate group," Trigg says. "We parked our motor homes together, but of course we were all sitting in different places in the stands during the game. So we set up a meeting place for after the game so we could get everyone together again, and when we got there someone suggested we go get corny dogs to celebrate the win.

"When we got to the corny dog stand there was this big, long line, so we gave all our tickets to a couple of guys to stand in the line and the rest of us were just hanging around waiting and talking about the game.

"So I'm over at the side talking to some people, and here come these two women, walking away from the stand, and one of them is really fussing, and she's saying, 'I'm not standing in this line—there's no corn dog in the world worth standing in that line.'

"As they walked by I just leaned out and said, 'You know what? You can only get a corn dog at the State Fair once a year, and this is the only place they're any good, so you ought to stand in line, because they're worth it.'

"They stopped and started talking, and so I took their tickets and gave 'em to my buddy in line and told him to get two more. Eventually he comes out with a big handful of corny dogs, and they took two of them and said, 'Thanks,' and walked off. And he says, 'Who the hell was that?' and I just said don't worry, they're paid for.

"So, about five or six hours later—after we'd done barbequing and everything—I fixed myself a drink and started walking around the RV lot. I walked over to a guy's motor home that I knew and I started telling him about these two crazy women we ran into at the corn dog stand. And this woman walks up and starts looking at me, and I turned to her and said, 'You look familiar.'

"And she says, 'Well, I'm the woman from the corn dog stand.'

"Turns out we both knew Doug, this guy I was talking to. It was pretty amazing—we ran into each other twice in the same afternoon, in the middle of 200,000 people. Two weeks later she came down to Austin to go to a football game with me, and we've been together ever since."

Rose, a registered dental hygienist, is one up on Trigg in at least one sense: she actually attended UT in the seventies before leaving to go to hygiene school and obtain her license.

Then there is JD, the dog.

"He's a stray," Trigg says. "My son-in-law found him when he was just a puppy and gave him to me. His name is JD, because the first time I saw him, I said, 'He's the same color as Jack Daniel's Whiskey.'

"Since then his color has changed to burnt orange. He's about two years old now, and he's a beautiful dog. He's an offshoot of a golden retriever; he looks like what they call a red golden retriever. But he's a great dog."

As far as life among the Rolling Horns is concerned, it would perhaps be insightful to look at it from the dog's perspective. "I'd had him for four days the first time I put him in the motor home and took him to a football game," Trigg says. "We've been traveling together ever since. As far as he's concerned, what life is all about is, you get into this big vehicle and drive somewhere, and when I open the doors he gets out and all his friends are there.

"He spends a few days with the people he's used to seeing, and if it's a road game there will be some new sights and smells. Then we get back in the vehicle and go home, and pretty soon we do the whole thing all over again.

"He probably thinks life is supposed to be this way. He doesn't know we're doing anything unusual."

A pretty fair description of the Rolling Horns, actually.

"It's basically just a group of friends who have motor homes who started hanging out together and going to the games over a period of time," Trigg says. "It's not like it was a big group of people who decided to think up a name and start a club. It started out with a few fans who wanted to tailgate together and just grew. People would come around and ask if they could join us, and the number of motor homes parked together just got larger.

"We've always been pretty open and laid back. We have people that are maybe 40 years old and others that are in their late seventies. Over time, it just evolved and got larger and larger. Finally some of the ladies started planning things ahead of time: They would contact everyone and say, 'OK, Friday we'll do sausages or bratwurst, or whatever, and everyone would bring something that went with it. It got to be kind of like a covered dish supper every night.

"We started contacting each other about road trips—where to park in Stillwater, things like that. Pretty soon, the e-mails were flowing back and forth. It got to be a lot of fun at road games because we would see new places and meet new people. And the night before the game, we would try to find out where all the locals went—like if you're in Stillwater, you go to Eskimo Joe's—and we'd go there, too. Maybe stir something up, just interact with people."

It is the general assessment that these trips have gone well. There was, however, one notable exception: "The worst place we've ever been," Trigg says, "is the trip last year to Columbus, Ohio. Those were just horrible, horrible people up there—mostly the students. The only place where I've ever felt physically threatened and in danger was on the streets of Columbus the night of the game. They wouldn't allow us to park on campus, so we used an RV park about 12 miles from the stadium. We decided to rent a limo van—with a TV and ice chest inside—and make a party of it. We also decorated it outside with several UT stickers.

"When we got down to the drag where the frat houses are, there were people and students in the street throwing things at the van—bottles, cans, whatever. They were cussing, hollering, trying to sling beer in through the windows, which we had opened.

"We finally got to a place where the police stopped the driver and told him he couldn't take it any further and we would have to get out. And one of [the police] told the driver, 'Get that thing the hell out of here—if you go any further you'll cause a riot.'

"The crowd just completely surrounded the van, and we told the police we had one guy who was in a wheelchair—so they backed the crowd away about 10 feet and we lifted him out.

"Then the driver closed the doors and drove away, and the cops just walked away and left us there in the middle of all those people. We were being cursed at and hollered at, and it was not a pleasant situation, but we finally got into the stadium. When we came out after the game—after we had won—nobody said a word to us."

The incident, however, has not diluted Trigg's fondness for the college football scene. "On the other hand," he says, "I love going to Nebraska, and a lot of it has to do with the people up there. They're classy people, and they're good football fans. They don't talk trash and treat you badly.

"In general, that's more the way it is. There are some people up in Chapel Hill, North Carolina, who sent us a congratulatory e-mail when they found out Rose and I were getting married, and another when we won the Rose Bowl. These are people we met at a football game seven or eight years ago.

"Most of the time, there's a common bond between college football fans ... a mutual respect."

The Rolling Horns, meanwhile, are still expanding. Having named themselves and created a website, Trigg says, "We negotiated with the Longhorn Foundation for a new parking area with electrical outlets so we don't have to run generators all the time."

They may have also found a way to while away those idle hours between football seasons. "A few years ago," he says, "a couple of us got together and found the exact halfway mark on the calendar between the end of the season and the beginning of the next, and we threw a 'Halfway to Kickoff Party' at my house. We sent out e-mails to everyone, because the whole group is scattered in several different cities.

"The night of the party, 60 people showed up. We had to find an RV park close by and just turn it into a long weekend party."

Meanwhile, the population inside Trigg's motor home has doubled. Where it was once just him and JD, it now includes Rose and her dog.

"I don't know exactly what kind he is," Trigg says, "but he's white. So now you've got two Longhorn fans with dogs that are burnt orange and white. They're both males, and they get along real well together. We call them 'The boys.'"

16

Wild Bunch

It was a pleasant spring afternoon at Disch-Falk Field, and as a special treat for the paying customers, a postgame brawl was in progress in the stands behind the visitors' dugout on the first-base side.

A few University of Houston baseball players, assorted girlfriends, and family members occupied one side of the debate. Arrayed against them and defending what had come to be considered their home turf were the rowdy, vocal, and unfailingly irreverent group of Texas fans known as The Wild Bunch.

In keeping with the tradition of the baseball melee, actual physical damage was slight. Several members of the invading force, however, withdrew with severely bruised feelings.

Across the field in the Texas dugout, centerfielder Joe Bruno watched the proceedings with growing admiration. Finally, he turned to his pal Ron Gardenhire and said, "You know, I'm really glad those guys are on our side."

There were other viewpoints, of course. Gazing upon a typical performance by the Wild Bunch, an opposing coach once said, "I wish I had my 12-gauge."

But Bruno's view was generally shared by longtime UT coach Cliff Gustafson, who had the benefit of Wild Bunch support for 20 years. He was certainly aware of their ability to offend the sensibilities of the less exuberant patrons, but he appreciated the effect they often had on Longhorn foes.

Articulate, informed, quick-witted, and thoroughly lubricated by frequent visits to the beer coolers in the parking lot, they could turn a trip to Disch-Falk into a survival course for the unwary. Entrenched in the

section of seats behind the visitor's dugout, they were loud and lewd …
and there was no place else they wanted to be.

Some of the best players in college baseball, at the end of a frustrating day, have honored them with a one-finger salute.

"It really all started a long time ago," says Scott Wilson, who has been the group's most recognizable member for 25 years. "I can remember back when they were still playing at Clark Field, there was a group of people who were doing this stuff—sitting together at the games, ragging the opponents, just having a good time. I didn't start sitting with them until they built Disch-Falk (1975).

"There were some world-class comedians in the group back then, and they did some really funny things. Then one day Kirk Bohls called us the Wild Bunch in the *Austin American-Statesman* and that's who we've been ever since—basically a bunch of rabid UT fans having fun." And in particular, getting in the mood to be rabid fans. In that regard, the Wild Bunch was blessed to have the patronage of the late Frank Erwin, generally regarded in his day to be the most powerful member of the Board of Regents. Erwin loved the Longhorns, hated the Aggies, and had no qualms about mixing those sentiments with a few social beverages. He and the Wild Bunch hit it off famously.

"We would always have several vehicles out in the parking lot, each with at least one beer cooler in it," Wilson says. "Sometimes after the games we would stay out there and party for hours. Frank wasn't much of a beer drinker—he preferred hard liquor—but he helped us get that tradition started. When the [university] police finally tried to evict us, Frank told them to leave us alone, and they did."

In recognition of this favor, the Wild Bunch established another tradition. "We always sat on the first-base side," Wilson says, "but Frank would sit over on the third-base side, behind the Longhorn dugout. So every game, when the visiting team was retired in the top of the fifth inning, we would all get up and yell, 'Hey Frank, it's the bottom of the fifth!' and he would raise up his glass and toast us with whatever he was drinking."

The tribute to Erwin was not the group's only contribution to Longhorn culture. Ask a Wild Bunch veteran what time it is, and you may get a rather distinctive answer:

"It's three o'clock, and OU sucks!"

This can continue all day: What time is it now? "It's eight thirty, and OU still sucks!"

This, however, was not the only activity the Wild Bunch could be counted on to perform reliably. The group's real value to the team was in the act of supporting—or sometimes starting—game-winning rallies.

It began with Wilson—whose cap is usually on backwards (rally-cap style) anyway—running up and down the stadium steps, getting people pumped up and making noise. He would then stand down in the aisle leading a rhythmic clapping and chanting by the crowd that steadily grew in volume to the point of being deafening.

This frequently had the effect of unnerving some members of the opposing force, and if perchance there was a muffed ball or errant throw, the din grew louder. Over the years, it was generally felt that a fair number of Longhorn rallies had been abetted by this performance.

Beyond that, the Wild Bunch played it for laughs.

They were known for performing elaborate pranks, such as marching into the stadium dressed in theme costumes. They formed their own kazoo band. At one point, they had their own air force, which came about in 1989 through the efforts of Wild Bunch members Jim Ryan and DeWaine Rice, who were builders of model airplanes, among other things.

That year, they built a remote-controlled craft that made three memorable flights before embarking on a brief film career.

The model plane first appeared, suddenly, from beyond an outfield wall at the Oklahoma game. Painted orange and white with "Go Longhorns" on the top and "OU Sux" on the bottom, it circled the field, buzzed several players, did a series of loops and rolls, and then flew back over the outfield wall and disappeared, while UT fans cheered wildly.

There was a repeat performance—with a logo change, for the A&M game—and a final flight in Omaha, at the College World Series, by which time the bottom logo simply read, "ESPN." The plane was later used in a movie, *Toy Soldiers.*

It was also against Oklahoma in '89 that the Wild Bunch made its most memorable entrance at a game. The OU football program at that time was having difficulties with the NCAA and various other authorities over off-the-field incidents that had cost coach Barry Switzer his job and eventually landed one Sooner star in prison.

In celebration of this circumstance, the Wild Bunch marched into Disch-Falk dressed in striped jail uniforms and then spent a full day taunting the Sooners. "For that one," Wilson says, proudly, "we made the *New York Times.*"

The same uniforms reappeared two years later for a game against Miami—whose football program was acquiring a widespread reputation for misbehavior on and off the field.

A few weeks earlier, in the course of a lopsided victory over the Longhorns, the Hurricanes had set a Cotton Bowl record for penalties. When the baseball team arrived at Disch-Falk, the Wild Bunch showed up in the convict uniforms—tossing yellow flags throughout the stands.

At most Longhorn games, the Wild Bunch found unique ways to busy itself. Prior to a College World Series game against Arkansas, the group barbequed a hog and marched into the stadium with its head on a pike.

The kazoo band made its first appearance at a game against Baylor— one of the nation's most prominent Baptist schools—when Wild Bunch members played hymns on the instruments. The Bears came and went, but the kazoos stayed—being used eventually to play theme music for Longhorn hitters.

At one game, a rather hefty umpire was approached on the field by a delivery person and was presented with a pizza, courtesy of the Wild Bunch.

On another occasion, an opposing hitter of ample girth drew the attention of several WB members, who used fishing poles to dangle doughnuts over the top of the dugout for him.

Occasionally, unsuspecting fans or relatives of the opposing team would seat themselves in the section behind the visitor's dugout—setting themselves up for a shock. Wild Bunch members—male and female— were noted for sharp-tongued barbs, and tempers soon reached a boil. This launched the melee witnessed by Bruno and Gardenhire … at the end of a game, a female Cougar fan stood up and threw a cup of water on a Wild Bunch member, who returned fire with a spit cup. No injuries were reported in the brief fray that followed, but it became a memorable WB moment.

Normally, however, the group was capable of appreciating the inspired riposte from a worthy foe. One such was Houston's Larry Coker, who once became so annoyed at the heckling of a female Wild Bunch member that he knotted a towel into the shape of a male appendage and flipped it back over the top of the dugout into her lap.

After the game, Coker was invited to join the Wild Bunch for a few beers in the parking lot, where he graciously autographed his creation for the lady in question.

But, as Wilson notes, the one foe the group could not ultimately overcome was time. Many of the original members are now "retired," and there have been few new additions over the years.

"Are we still a significant factor for the other team to worry about?" he says. "Probably not as much as we used to be. Nowadays we're a bunch of guys in our fifties or older, and we've slowed down. We don't party all night anymore, and it's not really the same, but we still have fun."

That was the whole point, all along, and the Wild Bunch certainly achieved its goal in unique fashion.

When a Wild Bunch reunion was organized several years ago, an information sheet was sent out to former members. Among other things, they were asked to list their most memorable experiences with the group.

One female member recalled an incident in which her "common decency" was questioned by an offended person.

"I never claimed to have any decency," she wrote. "And if I did, it certainly wouldn't be common!"

17

Orange-Minded Architect

For the past 16 years, Kenneth Lewis has made a good living building retail shopping centers in the Houston area, where he grew up.

Like many builders, he frequently tries to come up with new designs and concepts that will enhance the aesthetic effect of his creations, bringing more pleasing and enjoyable shopping days to his friends and neighbors.

So, as a civic-minded chap, Lewis has come up with an idea for something he feels will be the perfect addition to the local ambience. An idea, in fact, that may be long overdue. "We're designing a new shopping center right now that will have a unique feature," he says. "At night, I want to be able to light it up burnt orange whenever we win. Just like the tower in Austin."

"We," means the Texas Longhorns.

"It will be somewhere in the Houston area," he says. At the moment, the exact location remains vague. There may be Aggies out there who are armed and belligerent. If so, they will simply have to co-exist with Lewis, who is president of the local Longhorn Club, as they have for years. "I'm planning to do the same thing with the lights on my house," he says.

That hardly covers it. "I have a Longhorn tiled into my swimming pool," he says. "There's a basketball court in my backyard that is burnt orange, with a black Longhorn in the key. There is a life-size Longhorn topiary in the front yard—my wife gave me that for Father's Day last year. Inside the house there are quite a few UT-themed bronze statues. I have a customized license plate that says, 'UT Rules.'

"A few years ago, I bought a helmet on eBay that Ricky Williams had signed with "Heisman 98." So I sent it over to Austin and Earl Campbell signed it "Heisman 77."

There is a perfectly logical explanation for all of this, of course. "It's a sickness, I guess," he says.

If so, it's a condition of long standing. Lewis can trace it back to a Cub Scout meeting long ago, when the scoutmaster brought in Darrell Royal as a guest speaker. "I've been hooked at that point," he says, "and I've been a UT fan ever since.

"When I was in the fourth grade, my best friend was an Aggie," he says. "So in those days, every Thanksgiving I would tape little orange flags around my desk, and he would tape maroon flags around his. It was kind of neat.

"Also, when I was a kid, my parents' best friends from college lived in Little Rock, so every time the Arkansas game was played in War Memorial Stadium up there, my parents would send me up there as a birthday present, since my birthday was in October."

From there, Lewis went through Bellaire High School and the University of Texas—where he enrolled in the fall of 1977.

"My freshman year, we went undefeated, Earl Campbell won the Heisman Trophy, and we were ranked No. 1 going into the Cotton Bowl," he says. "I spent two nights camped out at the stadium. When they opened the ticket windows, I was the first in line."

It was a disaster—Notre Dame crushed the Longhorns, removing any consideration of a national title. For Lewis, however, it was a great year except for one game, and his support for the Longhorns has never wavered since. "We've had season tickets since I got out of high school," he says. "And ever since I got out of UT, I've been very heavily involved in the Alumni Association. I've been president of the Houston chapter of the Texas Exes, and now I'm with the Longhorn Club. The difference is that the Texas Exes is an alumni group and not actually part of the university, while the Longhorn Club is part of the university and is run through the Longhorn Foundation and the athletic department.

"There are about 40,000 alumni in Houston, with about 11,000 dues-paying families, while we have about 300 members in the Longhorn Club."

Any way you slice it, there are a lot of Longhorns, and a few years ago Lewis and some pals decided that maybe these folks needed a little more on their plate. Specifically, the thinking was that they all needed more barbeque. Thus was born an energetic little crew known as "Blowing Smoke."

It all has to do with a particular aspect of the Houston Livestock Show and Rodeo, a popular annual event that, Lewis felt, for many years had been overburdened with an Aggie influence. He felt it needed a dash of orange.

"I think the livestock show and rodeo actually goes on for about four weeks," he says, "but one part of it that goes on for the first three days is a barbeque cook-off event, and I think by now it's reached a point where there are about 400 to 500 teams competing every year.

"The stock show has always been heavily supported by the Aggies, and that included everything connected with it. They pretty much dominated it, and I felt we needed to create more of a Texas presence out there. So I got together with some friends of mine and we decided to form a barbeque cook-off team and enter the competition."

Which actually is not the simple matter it might appear to be. "Actually, it's very difficult," Lewis says. "There's a lot of competition for those cook-off spots, which are sponsored by local organizations or corporations, and getting in is almost impossible. Basically, you just about have to wait until someone dies before you can claim a spot.

"But we got lucky … an opportunity opened up when all of the cellular companies were changing hands. There was a lady in one barbeque booth whose sponsor fell out, and we were able to step in. I called all my UT alum buddies and corporations, and we put together a sponsorship and got a booth.

"The name of the team is 'Blowing Smoke,' and our logo is a Longhorn blowing smoke out of its nostrils. We also have quite a few other orange-themed things going on."

One of these—almost—was Bevo himself. "One year," Lewis says, "the [Silver] Spurs called and offered to bring Bevo out, and we thought it would be a great idea and would give us the best barbeque booth there. But the show officials denied the request, saying they didn't want live animals in that area because of safety concerns. I can see their point."

Competition is stiff, and there is a lot of hard work to be done, of course. The winners in each category receive belt buckles. "Basically," Lewis says, "it's a three-day party."

Somebody has to do it, and the ladies and gents of the Blowing Smoke brigade have generally acquitted themselves well. "Usually, we'll do brisket, ribs, and chicken," Lewis says, "a lot of it. I think every year we've finished in the top 10 or 15 percent overall. It's hard to win with 500 teams out there, but we've come in first in some of the side competitions.

"We've won 'Recycling' … which means we drank more beer than anyone else. And we've won 'Cleanest Booth.'

"Actually, the people with the hardest job are the judges. Can you imagine tasting 500 of any of those, and trying to pick which is best?"

Who actually eats all of this?

"The sponsors get to invite guests," he says. However, in Lewis' estimation, the big achievement is that the original objective is being realized: there is now a large and growing Texas presence at the stock show each year. "Most of the people out there are Aggies," he says, "but we fly UT flags, and we've gotten more and more of our alums involved every year. This includes a lot of the alums who are big donors and are coming out now to give support.

"Now, each year there's a University of Texas Night at the rodeo."

Elsewhere, Lewis works diligently to keep the home fires burning … orange.

He and his wife, Stacy, have been married three years. They met in the Texas Exes organization. Lewis has four children—three from a previous marriage—and it is a sure bet that Andrew (18), Allison (16), Sarah (8) and Sophie (1), have their feet firmly placed on the Orange Brick Road.

"The two oldest ones have been going to Longhorn games since they were one or two years old," he says. He keeps an open mind about the future, of course.

"I've been telling all of them since they were old enough to speak," he says, "that education is the most important thing and they can go to college wherever they want to. But … I've also told them that I will not pay for Oklahoma, and I will not pay for Notre Dame. If they choose to go to A&M, I'll probably pay for it … but I may not visit them. I still haven't been to the Bush Library over there."

The message seems to be sinking in; Lewis fondly recalls a conversation he had with his oldest daughter several years ago. "We were driving back home from a game in Austin," he says, "and she was probably about seven or eight then. We were talking and she said, 'Dad, I think I want to be a veterinarian, because I really love animals.'

"I told her that was great, and I said, 'You know, the best veterinary school in this part of the country is at Texas A&M.'

"After that, there was a long silence, and finally she said, 'Well Dad, I guess I don't really have to be the best vet there is.'"

Regardless of where everyone winds up, one thing is for certain—by the time they're out of high school, they will have seen a lot of Longhorn football.

"We will usually go to every home game," Lewis says, "and we'll also try to go on the road to the marquee game of that year. When we go to

Austin early in the year, we'll usually stay overnight and take the kids out on the lake. Later in the year we'll go just for the game. Usually we'll tailgate at the Alumni Center because it's so convenient and they do a great tailgate."

The road schedule includes the annual trek to the Cotton Bowl for the OU game, something Lewis has been doing since he was in college and the rest of the family has done for as long as they can remember.

Although Lewis is not particularly distressed at the idea that the game might be moved out of Dallas, he says his family will be there every year as long as it is. "I know that there is a view that the existing situation has certain negatives," he says, "such as the game being a prime recruiting tool for Oklahoma. If it is moved, so be it. But until then, we'll go.

"Our kids know the rule: if our team is down there on the field, we're up in the stands, no matter what the weather is. We've sat through some drenching downpours up there but we've never left. And no matter how the game goes, we stay till the end."

It is permissible to avoid certain road venues. "I've been to Waco," he says, as if recalling a trip where he took a wrong turn, "and we will typically skip Stillwater and Lubbock, but we've been to a lot of places that were truly memorable. The fans at Nebraska are always impressive— really great fans. The same is true at Notre Dame—even though we lost the game, it was a very worthwhile experience because they have such great fans. And we had a wonderful college experience at Virginia, even though, again, we lost."

Lewis also made the Ohio State trip last year: a tremendous victory for the Longhorns, and a mixed blessing for the fans. "The game was fun, but their fans were terrible," he says. "They were yelling and cursing at everyone … and grabbing their crotch and making obscene gestures at the women, regardless of age. There was a lot of controversy afterward, and I think their president wrote a letter of apology to UT."

The situation was a perfect opportunity, of course, to wave the orange flag again.

"In the Texas Exes," he says, "there is a Committee on Sportsmanship, and there have been discussions about that game, and how to handle their visit to Austin this year. It's important to us to make sure that when they come down here, they don't have to go through the same thing we did up there.

"To me, that is a big part of what it means to be a Texas grad and a Texas fan."

John Gilbert, 49, a Houston real estate developer and one of Lewis' close friends, also lays claim to having orange blood—he's just a little less noticeable. "I have tons of orange T-shirts, sweat shirts and caps," he says, laughing, "but if I went any farther than that, my wife would kill me."

Then again, maybe not. He and his wife Julie—a former features editor and writer at the old *Houston Post*—met at UT, graduated together ('79), and have sent both of their kids to their alma mater.

Jeffrey got an undergraduate degree in journalism, with honors, and is now in his first year at UT law school. Amy is a freshman majoring in psychology. Both—like their father—grew up going to Longhorn games.

"Both of my parents went to school there," Gilbert says, "and my dad hardly ever missed a game. We go to the home games and try to make some of the road games."

And like Lewis, he has been known to wave the Longhorn flag in hostile territory.

"I went up to Columbus this year, and it was quite a trip," he says. "I have a cousin who lives up there, and he got us booked into the Holiday Inn on campus. Everybody had all their Ohio State stuff on, so I hung my Texas flag in the window.

"The day of the game, there were thousands of people down there tailgating and partying all day long. It was really funny—every time I looked out the window, there were all these people down there shooting me the bird.

"When it started getting close to game time, it was looking more like a Rolling Stones concert down there—girls were getting up on guys' shoulders and ripping their tops off—it was really wild.

"What really amazed me was that in addition to the 100,000 who went to the game, there must have been 75,000 who didn't even have tickets. They just came to party all day. For me, the only trip that topped that was the Rose Bowl."

In fact, the whole scene kind of brought back memories of his youth … and Texas-OU weekend in Dallas. "It would really be a crime if they ever take that game out of Dallas," he says. "It's a unique game, a great tradition, and in spite of the cost of renovating the Cotton Bowl, I still think it's worth it to everyone concerned."

There was also a time when it was a grand party … where up and down Commerce Street, the common folk mingled with the mighty, and everyone pretty much wound up in the same shape.

Where an impressionable college youth might run into, say—the governor. Take part in meaningful dialogue, so to speak.

"The trip I'll never forget was in 1977," Gilbert says. "Both teams ranked in the top five, and we were up there partying all Friday night, like everyone else. Several of us rented a room at the Adolphus, on Commerce, and about 2 a.m. we came back to the lobby and headed up to bed. The elevator door was closing, but we stuck a foot in the door and got in.

"We got on the elevator—and there was Dolph Briscoe, the governor. Two state troopers were holding him up, and they all looked pretty surprised to see us. Immediately, we started talking to him about the previous year—when the game ended in a 6–6 tie and they had a coin flip to see which team got the trophy, and he lost.

"We gave him crap about that the whole way up in the elevator."

18

DAVID SQUIRE

President of the Dallas Texas Exes

When it comes to pure, undiluted, pedal-to-the-metal, burning orange devotion to the Texas Longhorns, David Squire is a hard man to beat. Also, as current president of the Dallas chapter of the Texas Exes, he is perfectly positioned to advance the cause and fan the flames of patriotism in a major metropolis.

Of course, like any other massive urban population center, Dallas can be a dangerous place, and we are not talking about street gangs here. Anyone who has experienced the thrill of regularly traversing the area's myriad freeway systems has a fair notion of what it might have been like to be a World War II fighter pilot.

"I get really, really upset when someone cuts me off in traffic," Squire says. "When that happens, I will definitely sit there and cuss that person. Except when I see that they have a Longhorn sticker on their car. Then I stop. Just the fact that we both walked the Forty Acres once means that I have something very special in common with that person."

Such generosity of the soul, of course, would seem to indicate that in his devotion, Squire knows no equal.

Except for his wife, Misty.

After all, how often has it been recorded that a bride has specifically included it in her wedding vows that she would be "The best Longhorn wife ever"? This coming from a young woman who had grown up as an admirer of the, um, Aggies.

"All his buddies loved it," she says, laughing, "but I really feel that way—once I was exposed to it, I just totally embraced it."

Given their double devotion, it is fortunate that the Squires—rising young professionals—have few job conflicts. They both work for Merrill Lynch. David, 36, is a financial advisor and certified financial planner in the Arlington office, and Misty, 31, is a registered client associate in a Dallas office.

But these are only aliases … whenever possible, they are both decked out in orange tailgating with friends, working in the Dallas chapter and supporting the Longhorns from Austin to Pasadena.

Oddly, neither comes from a UT family, although David—who grew up in Garland—attended UT and came out with a degree in finance in '91. Misty grew up in East Texas and never gave the Longhorns a thought until she ran into a whirlwind courtship.

"I grew up in Lindale and went to Tyler JC, originally to study nursing," she says, "but by 1998 I had changed careers. The company I worked for had offices in Tyler and Longview, and they alternated each year on the Christmas party.

"David was working for the same company in Dallas, and he and his buddies had decided to drive to Shreveport to do some gambling on the riverboats. One of his friends was the son of the guy giving our Christmas party in Longview, and on the way back from Shreveport they decided to stop in for a free beer.

"That's how we met, and when they left that night he told his friends he was going to marry me."

They got married in '99 ("I knew what I wanted," he says) and Misty soon learned that it was sort of a double wedding. She got David and the Longhorns. "I had never cared anything about Texas before we met," she says. "In fact, when I was growing up I loved the Aggies, because my basketball coach—my mentor, actually—had gone to A&M.

"In fact, when we were cleaning out my old house he found a Polaroid of me wearing an Aggie sweatshirt, and there was also a Texas

A&M banner. He was going to keep it and burn it at one of the games, but we ended up just throwing it away."

David played football and basketball at South Garland High School and is not sure why he became a Longhorn fan. "My father was from Michigan and came down here when he got a job at Texas Instruments," he says, "and my stepfather—who had been with us since I was eight—was an Oklahoma State grad. In fact, he was the Pistol Pete mascot back in '63, and his daughter—my stepsister—went to OSU.

"I latched onto the Longhorns as a young kid and followed them intently. I think it was probably just because it was the state university and I'm such a proud Texan. I've always been very loyal to that."

Although he also applied to Arizona State, he quickly forgot about it ("I don't even know whether I was accepted or not") and arrived at UT in '87. "My four years on campus back then were pretty much just studying," he says, "and I really didn't get much involved in extracurricular activities beyond intramural sports.

"Back at that time at Texas, we were pretty bad, and it really wasn't a lot of fun. There wasn't that much tailgating. There weren't that many students who went to the games. We did go, but there weren't a lot of us. I started in '87, and we went to the Cotton Bowl in 1990—we were actually OK that year, but we got just dismantled by Miami in the Cotton Bowl."

After graduation, Squire came back to Dallas—and discovered a new influence in his life. "It seemed like the natural thing to do was to get involved with the Exes," he says, "but I really don't know what the catalyst for that was, because most people don't. The vast majority get involved in their professional lives and never think about it.

"I wasn't specifically about meeting people—but once I got involved, seeing the things they do, I realized there was a lot of opportunity there to meet people who share your values and to get involved with community service. In general, the goal of the chapter is to provide the opportunity to bring our alumni base together in whatever atmosphere there is.

"In our particular chapter we have a scholarship endowment where we raise funds for scholarships for high school seniors in the Dallas area."

Although not a UT grad, Misty says she "became a true Longhorn fan," after they were married.

"Of all the Dallas Longhorn wives, I've jumped in and volunteered from Day One," she says. "I take my vacation days in ways that allow me to be involved in it, and I spend a lot of my time doing volunteer work connected with it. Sometimes he may not be able to go to a particular event, and I'll go in his place. One of us is always there.

"I've been sold on it ever since the first time he took me to a football game at UT. It was just unbelievable. I loved it."

One of the big events for the chapter is the annual March 2 Texas Independence celebration. There is also, of course, Texas-OU weekend.

"It starts Thursday night with our 'Burnt Orange Blast-Off' where we get a local establishment—usually a bar—to host a party," he says. "Basically a Happy Hour bash.

"Friday morning we have our annual golf tournament, which is one of the largest alumni golf tournaments in the country. Last year we sold it out and had 301 golfers. We play at Firewheel in Garland, 36 holes on two courses. We have prizes, gifts, and raffles—tickets to the game, airline tickets, trips to Mexico. The proceeds go to our scholarship fund.

"That night we have the 'Bash Before The Clash,' which was originally a street party. We used to set up tents in the streets with live bands, but now it's more or less evolved into a party over at the Iron Cactus restaurant, and they pretty much run it for us."

From his student days, he recalls that "five or six or even 10 of us would come up and get a cheap hotel room and do Commerce Street on Friday night, and it was a sad day when they shut that down—but towards the end it got real dangerous down there.

"It was amazing. You'd see people with these big trash cans on wheels full of ice and beer, and they would have ropes tied around their waists and they'd pull those trash cans up and down the street. Obviously, a lot of people were very drunk.

"But I don't think the rivalry has changed … I think 90 percent are just people who enjoy their school and are out to have fun. You have the 10–15 percent—on both sides—who are confrontational and looking for a fight. We never got in a fight up there … one time one of my buddies went off into an alley to relieve himself and some guy came up and ripped the chain off his neck and took his wallet. But that was about the time street gangs started showing up, so it's probably a good thing they shut it down."

Misty's main Texas-OU memory is a bus ride.

"One of his friends used to rent a bus, and we would go bar-hopping," she says. "There would be food and drink beforehand—then we'd put a keg on the bus and go to OU bars, Texas bars, the whole thing. It was really fun."

Like any civic-minded gent, Squire has definite feelings about the future of the Texas-OU game: keep it where it is.

"Well, from the standpoint of the Dallas Texas Exes," he says, "this weekend is what drives our entire chapter's ability to do what it does. We made a $50,000 contribution to our endowment fund this year, and $30,000 of it came from the Texas-OU weekend events.

"From a pure fan perspective, they have to keep it here: it's unique. There's something special about it that can't be duplicated (home and home), and I don't think you can pick it up and move it to the new Cowboy stadium in Arlington. It's unique to the downtown area, unique to the State Fair, unique to the two schools. It's one of a kind.

"The Cotton Bowl? Nobody has complained more about that stadium than I have—the entire upper deck, where we sit, is serviced by one women's restroom. But the city of Dallas needs to do whatever is necessary to get the ADs of the two schools to sign a long-term agreement to keep it here."

On the other hand, there is the A&M game, which is a trip to Austin every other year. Or perhaps a lifestyle. "I had to tell my parents six years ago," Misty says, "that I couldn't spend Thanksgiving with them anymore."

Squire and his friends make annual forays to College Station when the Aggies are hosting—but they don't leave until around 5 p.m. Thanksgiving day for a game the next day. When the game is in Austin, preparations are more elaborate and are now augmented by a new acquisition the Squires came up with several years ago—an RV.

The couple fell in with a group of RV enthusiasts known as the Rolling Horns, and as a result, home games in Austin now feature all the comforts of home—and the tailgate goes on around the clock. "The main thing is, the parking is so competitive that although the game is Friday, you have to get down there Wednesday night to get a spot," Misty says. "Basically, as soon as you get off work on Wednesday, you pack up and go."

Turkey is an obvious choice for the A&M game, but, Squire says, the culinary theme among the group normally differs from game to game. "Last year we got down there Wednesday night and set up the RV and then started deep-frying turkeys on Thanksgiving morning," he says. "But usually there's a different theme from game to game, whether it's breakfast, brisket, hamburgers, pork loin or whatever. Shrimp and chicken wrapped in bacon with jalapenos is popular."

Although most have a satellite dish for TV, one of Squire's pals has pretty much cranked the comfort level to the max. "Every time he rolls in," Squire says, "he sets up two huge tents and brings out his 60-inch Sony flat-screen HD television, with surround-sound speakers set up all around the tents. In fact, he watches the game from there."

There is, however, a method to this madness, Misty says. "There are a lot of people at the tailgate who don't have tickets for the game, so when he sets up to watch the game, he usually has 25 to 35 people in the tent with him. "We usually go into the stadium for the game. David has to be in his seat when they come out of the tunnel, and he won't leave until they play 'The Eyes of Texas' ... even if the score is 70–3."

Basically, your standard easy-living lifestyle, enlivened by the occasional trip to the emergency room.

"One time," Squire says, "I was putting some wood on a guy's smoker for him, and I opened the door to the smoker—this big, huge cast-iron door—and after I put the wood in I thought to myself, 'You know, David, that handle is probably going to be very hot.' So I just tried to push the door shut, but I put my hand on that hot iron."

He was soon at the local emergency room with second-degree burns.

"They wouldn't give me any kind of pain medication," he says, "because I had obviously had a few cocktails. I just told them to make sure I was out of there in time for the kickoff."

As Misty recalls, "We finally got out of there about 4 a.m. The main thing I remember about it was there were these two guys next to us who had obviously been in a fight. They were pretty mangled. Turns out they were best friends and had gotten into an argument and beat each other up. But they made up before we left.

"The emergency room staff was not amused at all. On the night before the A&M game, they get a little short on sympathy.

"But I did enjoy going to yell practice. I couldn't believe that the Aggies hold yell practice in Austin the night before the game—on the steps of the state capitol—surrounded by heckling UT fans. But it was fun."

The RV thing, Squire says, sort of came up as a matter of necessity a few years ago.

"For years, we used to tailgate on the roof of a parking garage next to Scholtz's, and then we moved to another one across the street. It got to

where the more we did that, the longer we wanted to stay, and the more
we wanted to do, and the bottom line was, the wives and girlfriends were
spending most of their time in long lines for the restroom. So finally I
said, 'This is crazy—let's get an RV.'

"Everybody thought I was crazy, but I looked in an Austin paper
after a game once, and found an attorney that had a used one for sale. He
quoted what I thought was a reasonable price, I offered him a little bit
less, and we made a deal."

The first RV was a 1988 Pace Arrow, which was fun but unreliable.
"We really loved it, but it finally broke down," he says. "So I traded it in
on a 1995 Jako Eagle and we've been driving that for the past few years.
It's still kind of mauve and blue, but this summer I'm going to get it
painted up in orange. We've driven it to games at Nebraska, Lubbock,
Baylor, OSU, and up to the College World Series, and we've really
enjoyed it.

"Meeting the people in the Rolling Horns has been quite a trip, too.
A lot of them have new, really expensive RVs and they travel all over the
country and meet at games. You can always spot them together, because
each has a Texas flag above a Longhorn flag, with an iron longhorn on top
of the flagpole."

On matters pertaining to the Longhorns, about the only point of
disagreement between the Squires is on selecting the most intense rivalry.

For Misty, whose frame of reference dates back to '99, it's Oklahoma.
David, who remembers the lean years of the eighties and early nineties,
remains eternally wary of the Aggies.

As for what it means to be a Longhorn fanatic, the duo is pretty
much in the same pew. "I've never been a part of anything before that has
so much tradition behind it," Misty says. "To me, it's just a blast being a
Longhorn fan. It's just all the different things that go into it. The very first
football game he took me to, I was almost speechless at the entire thing.
There's so much love from the fans—whether they went to school there
or not—and it's just a lot of fun.

"I've got friends or people I work with that went to school there that
are not into it as much as I am; I'm a lifetime member now, and I'll always

love the Longhorns. This is something we can enjoy together ... whether it's a Texas Exes function or a tailgate or going to an event or what. It's just great."

David notes that, "Sports is one of the things I've always gravitated toward as an outlet for ... just about everything. I never got deeply involved in professional sports other than an interest in the Cowboys or Rangers or whatever, because they're here.

"When it comes to Texas, it's just the experience you gain from being there and the opportunities it has created in my life—something that I really treasure. I feel like I owe it not only to the university but to all the kids that are going to go through that experience to make sure that I give something back, and that there are other people out there who can benefit.

"What's important about the Texas Exes is ... everybody has their own reason for doing volunteer work. For me, the biggest reason is that I value the diploma that I have and I want to continue to raise its value— the bar has already been raised to the point that I probably couldn't get in there now with the scores I had then, and I want to see it continue that way. [It] translates into what is probably the biggest social outlet in this neck of the woods—sports.

"It's nice to have something that is bigger than yourself that you can hold onto and believe in—and to try to make it better. Outside of religion, I don't know where else you're going to find that."

19

The Hellraisers

When Jeff Hattendorf and his companions left the stadium after Texas' crucial victory over Ohio State last fall in Columbus, they were suddenly confronted by a group of Buckeye fans. However, in contrast to several other reports from that particular road trip, this was a happy encounter. The hosts were gracious and friendly.

In fact, they almost seemed awestruck. "They were really nice," Hattendorf says. "They invited us to their tailgate and gave us a beer, and we just sat around talking about the game and the trip, and they mentioned they were going to Cleveland the next day for the Browns game ... and they're talking to us like, 'Wow, you've got the Cowboys down there.'

"And I'm like, the Cowboys? Hey, I've got the Longhorns, that's who I've got. The Cowboys can win all the Super Bowls they want, but I don't really care. I just want Texas to win a national championship—and that's the only thing that matters to me."

Mission accomplished—eventually.

The attitude of rather singular purpose is something Hattendorf, 36, has carried through most of his adult life—ever since he left Lamar High School in Arlington and enrolled at UT in the late eighties. "We went through a very long and painful dry spell when I was a student there," he says. "There was that one bright, shining year in 1990 when we got to the Cotton Bowl, and I was so excited. [But] then the game was basically over by halftime.

"You have to figure it's a bad sign when your return man takes the opening kickoff, gets knocked down, gets up, goes three wobbly steps, and then falls down again. I felt sorry for him, but it sure didn't get any better after that.

"I've been to over 100 UT games, and that was one of three where I've left early," he says. "I don't leave just because they're behind. In fact, they can be way behind and I'll stick with them as long as they're in there fighting. But when the team quits, I quit ... and that's sure what it looked like that day."

Fortunately, he hasn't had to make a habit of it. But Hattendorf, a 1992 UT grad now back in Arlington with a new firm, Microspect, has been forced to alter his enthusiasm (slightly) in recent years. He and his wife, Holly—who he met in graduate school at TCU—have two new family additions: Ashley, 4, and Zach, 1.

"We've been married eight years," he says. "We stayed here after grad school, but we still went down to Austin for all the home games, until Zach was born. My poor daughter got dragged to all those games when she was little, but after Zach came, it didn't make sense to drag two of them down there for every game."

However, Jeff still manages to see most of them. "Holly is from Nebraska. In fact, she grew up in Lincoln," he says, "but fortunately she wasn't a die-hard Cornhusker fan. She came down here because TCU has a really strong recruiting program. So right now my kids know three things: Texas, Nebraska, and TCU, but I'm getting them started as Longhorn fans."

The pursuit comes naturally for Hattendorf, who is also active in the Texas Exes chapter in Dallas. And long ago, when he became disappointed with the fan intensity level at UT, he took bold, decisive action. He became a hellraiser.

More particularly, he became a member of a new group on campus that called itself The Longhorn Hellraisers. They may not always make the list of officially sanctioned "spirit" groups at UT, but anyone who has watched a Longhorn football game over the past 20 years—particularly a televised one—has met them.

Usually situated in a corner of the end zone, they are the screaming, howling, orange-painted students that the cameras zoom in on when there is a commercial break. Tongues wagging, caps on backward, they seem—just for a moment—to have landed in your living room with a "HOOK 'EM!" message for you.

"I joined in the spring of my freshman year, which was about the second or third year after they started," Hattendorf says. "Ironically, the organization was started by a couple of guys who had transferred in from LSU and Michigan.

"The LSU guy was Kevin Marcentell—who I think is now an assistant district attorney in El Paso—and I can't remember the other guy's name. Anyway, they were pretty disappointed with the fan enthusiasm when they got here, so they decided to come up with something that would get people pumped up and increase fan participation. They formed the Longhorn Hellraisers to get people more into the game and more vocally supporting the team."

The idea wasn't entirely embraced with enthusiasm at all levels. "For a long time," Hattendorf says, "I think the attitude of the administration could be described as benign neglect. I think basically there was a problem with the name Hellraisers, which was not very well thought of at that level. Even today, when you go to games you still don't see the group listed among the spirit organizations … but they get great front-row seats."

Hattendorf admits that in the beginning, the effort may have exuded the aura of wasted energy. "Our enthusiasm may have exceeded the level of competition at times," he says, laughing. "I still have vivid memories of a game where we beat North Texas because of an end-zone call by the official that I'm sure their fans are bitter about to this day. But we always tried to make every game seem like a big game.

"We all wore white shirts and painted our faces burnt orange and put on the 'rally caps' whenever the offense got into the red zone. Actually, for a while it seemed like [the Longhorns] kicked so many field goals in that situation that we developed a special cheer indicating we preferred touchdowns. In the beginning, [the Hellraisers] were all guys, but they've gone coed now.

"When I was in school, we made a point of going to at least one event for every sport on campus. We went to several baseball games, all the home basketball games, and every home football game.

"When I was there, we usually had between 30 and 60 guys, depending on the semester and the year. Usually in the fall, everyone wanted to be a Hellraiser, and then you would lose a lot of guys in the spring. So we'd do a big recruiting push and build up for the next fall."

Soon, there was a standard routine for football games. "Before the game," Hattendorf says, "we would get together in someone's apartment or dorm room, paint our faces up, and have a little party. Then we would make our run to the stadium. We would walk over from the west side of the campus to that hill that leads down to Belmont, and from there we would sprint into the stadium.

"At the games, we were loud, animated, and obnoxious. Whenever it got quiet—if the cheerleaders weren't doing a cheer and we figured it was time for one, we would start it. We also started a routine where we would get the smallest guy in the group, and after every score we would push him up as many times as we had points on the board, and the crowd would keep score with a chant.

"From what I've been seeing lately, now sometimes they push up the ESPN guy.

"One of my favorite games of all time was that 1990 game against Houston where we beat them so bad, and it was such a relief after all those 60–40 games we had lost to them. I think late in the third quarter or early in the fourth, we all took out our car keys and started jingling them— meaning this game's over and it's time to go start the bus. We started that, and they still do that today."

Despite a growing reputation as the school's official rowdies, Hattendorf recalls, there was a strict limit on what they could say and do at games. "One thing we always had to abide by—because the university was keeping an eye on official spirit organizations, or the sanctioned ones—was that you could not alter the words [of] any chant or fight song," he says. "That 'Give 'em hell, give 'em hell' chant—if you actually repeated what the rest of the students were putting on the end of it, you could lose your place in life.

"I'm sure a lot of people probably thought we were a little weird, but I don't think we ever had an outlaw rep or anything like that. I think people mostly understood that we were just going to show up at games and be loud and heckle the other team—within reason."

In fact, the group soon had a prominent unofficial sponsor—head basketball coach Tom Penders, who displayed a picture of the Hellraisers on his office wall. "When we first started going to the games," Hattendorf says, "we sat way up in the upper section, and pretty soon Penders looked up and saw all these guys up there with orange faces, yelling at the opposition—and he promptly had us moved down to the section right behind the basket.

"For the rest of my time at UT, that's where I sat for basketball games. Each year, he would put a current Hellraiser photo on his wall, but the very first one he ever hung up there, I was in it."

Meanwhile, life was meant to be enjoyed, and the Hellraisers were acutely aware of their responsibilities in this regard. In fact, at the baseball games the Wild Bunch soon befriended them. "They kind of adopted us," Hattendorf says. "At the baseball games we just kind of followed their lead and supported them, and we got invited to all their parties."

Not that the Hellraisers were incapable of fending for themselves.

"Well, one thing we started doing was having a campout every spring, where we'd spend about 36 hours camped out at the lake," he says. "But also, we were definitely having a party after every football game. We didn't have a frat house, so we had to find someplace—an apartment, a club, something—and we'd throw a party after every home game. Those things use to amaze me. We had like 40 guys in the group, and 500 people would show up for the party.

"The places we used, sometimes they would let us come back, sometimes they wouldn't let us come back."

The OU weekend also proved entertaining, on and off the field.

"We always used to go up to Dallas and do Commerce Street," Hattendorf says. "We never got in a fight, but we did have a tense situation once right after the game. We were coming out of the stadium after another win—seems like we always beat OU because we had Peter Gardere—and we were painted up and screaming and yelling, 'OU sucks!'—hey, it's a tradition. They do the same thing when they win. But there was a crowd of OU guys there and they didn't want to hear any more of it, and they moved around and blocked our path.

"We were both ready to have a fight right there, but eventually cooler heads prevailed. Things calmed down, and we moved on around them and went on our way."

This was actually less stressful, he says, than the "profanity-laced tirade I got my freshman year from a woman on Commerce Street who was about 50 or 60 years old, dealing with my family history and my mother and grandmother and various sexual acts. Actually, she was probably younger than that, but I was 18 and she looked really old.

"Oh yeah … she was wearing red."

Of the two major UT rivals, in fact, Hattendorf regards the Sooners as being much stranger than the Aggies. "They're both big rivals," he says, "but with a difference. To me, OU is like the kid down the street that you don't like—you want to whip them every time you play them, and you want them to get whipped every time they play someone else. The Aggies are more like my younger brother. I want to whip him every time we compete, but when he's out doing something else, I cheer for him as much as I can.

"In fact, there's an interesting thing about the OU rivalry—I see this a lot when I go up to Nebraska to visit my wife's family. Driving through Oklahoma, you will see car after car with an upside down Longhorn sticker on it—and not a single OU sticker on the car.

"They hate Texas more than they love OU."

Not that the Aggies have been immune, traditionally, from pranks pulled off by Hattendorf and his friends. "One year," he says, "I had a roommate who was Navy ROTC, and during some kind of joint military gathering, he stole the Guide-On from one of the Aggie units. We had it in our apartment, with one of their helmets, for about 18 months. They finally came to our door and asked for it back. It seems they had been told that they wouldn't be allowed to graduate unless they got it back."

If OU fans are a bit strange, Hattendorf figures he encountered a lot worse at Ohio State—despite the festive group of Cowboy enthusiasts who hosted him after the game. "I went to Notre Dame once," he says, "and since they're the Cowboys of college football, with their own network and all, I figured those fans would be really arrogant. But they couldn't have been nicer to us—they were very friendly and helpful.

"In Columbus, the game itself was spectacular. There had been so much hype about it; how the entire Texas team was pointing at that game and had been ever since the ('05) Rose Bowl. It was such a great win for us, and it was definitely worth the trip. But in so many instances, the fans were very different from the ones at Notre Dame. We definitely met a lot of good fans up there, but a higher percentage of them were confrontational and looking for a fight.

"Fortunately, we didn't go to the High Street area—a long stretch where there are bars on one side of the street and frat houses on the other, and there are a lot of fights. But it kind of tells you something … the band didn't come to our pregame tailgate because the local police told them they could not protect them on the quarter-mile walk to the stadium from the hotel.

"One of the TV analysts even said that High Street had become a sort of crime-ridden area, including a lot of people in the pregame atmosphere who weren't going to the game. All in all, it was a disappointment."

Closer to home, Hattendorf has rediscovered his first allegiance—the Lamar Vikings, his old high school team. Unfortunately, he has also discovered that he is a jinx. "We never made the playoffs the three years I was in high school, but they've made it every year except two since I left," he says. "But when I started going to their playoff games, four years in a row, I ended their season. So now I just go to district games. I stay out of the playoffs."

As for his other team …

"It used to be," he says, "that when Texas lost, I felt that I had lost. I would be frustrated beyond belief.

"There are still times when I get frustrated, but I have a perspective on it now. It's easier now that they're winning a lot. It used to be [that] I had to see every game. I don't now, but when I do go, I always have to be in my seat at the kickoff. That's my responsibility as a fan.

"I wear my colors—win or lose. To me, you can be a fan—whether you went to school there or not—if you stick with them through thick and thin. That's what matters.

"I've been through all the thin times. Now I'm enjoying some of the thick times."

And the Hellraisers?

"Well, it's probably once a Hellraiser, always a Hellraiser," he says. "I have a bunch of friends from that time, and we still get together and tailgate to this day.

"We don't paint our faces anymore. We're a little old for that now."

20

The Flying Longhorns

After 17 years of directing traffic for a band of globetrotters known as the "Flying Longhorns," Betty Cotten admits that not quite every remote corner of the planet piques her interest.

"I've never been to Antarctica," she says. "Nor will I go."

This probably puts her right in step with about 98.7 percent of the people who ever thought about it to begin with, but for Cotten—the ultimate flyer—there's a specific reason.

"The closest you can get by plane is Argentina," she says. "Then you have to take a boat across the Drake Passage—one of the most notorious bodies of water in the world. You can have 30-foot waves on a clear day, and I'm just afraid to try it.

"I get very seasick."

But that's about the only problem that Betty—the wife of Austin attorney and former UT football great Mike Cotten—has ever had with the job. In fact, apart from having to catch *March of the Penguins* on the tube, she can reasonably feel that the rest of the planet is her world.

As for exotic locales, her favorite thus far is Myanmar, which the less current among us probably still refer to as Burma. "I went there on a personal trip, and I absolutely loved that country," she says. It's very soft and the people are lovely, and there are so many wonderful archeological sites."

Cotten says she "sort of fell into the job when my children went to college and I started thinking, 'Hey, maybe I'll get a job.' I was 45 years old and had always been a wife and mother and community volunteer, and I had never had any prior experience working as a travel agent.

"I had just always been a very committed traveler. I love to travel, and to me, seeing the world is the best way you can spend your time. It's been a wonderful experience, and I've met a lot of incredibly wonderful people."

Through the years, both Cotten and the Flying Longhorns have expanded their horizons considerably. "The Flying Longhorns is a group travel program of the Texas Exes that began in 1961," she says. "In those days, it involved charter flights to Europe. The routine was just 'fill a plane and take off'. Of course, there wasn't as much travel then as there is now.

"It has evolved over the years, and now we do about 35 to 40 trips per year. Generally, we will have at least one trip a year that goes to a football game. Last year, the trip was to Ohio State.

"We always try to pick a trip to a place a lot of people are interested in going to ... we went up to the Rutgers game a few years ago, we went to San Francisco when we played Stanford, and to Los Angeles when we played UCLA. We flew close to 200 people up to the Rutgers game and there were over 100 who went with us to Ohio State. Everybody seems to have a good time, and it's been a lot of fun.

"We also go to bowl games ... the last two years we've taken about 1,000 people to the Rose Bowl. Those have been really fun trips.

"We also do some bus trips. We take about six busses up to Dallas for the OU game each year. We drive up there Saturday morning ... in time to spend a couple of hours at the State Fair. Then we come back to Austin immediately after the game. I've had a lot of people tell me that's the best way to see the OU game.

"We've also started something new within the last few years—we partner with men's athletics and the band and cheerleaders for game-day charters. For road games, the band usually takes a smaller contingent of about 50, plus 12 cheerleaders, and they don't fill a Southwest (Airlines) charter.

So we buy into that, and that way we've gone to some Big 12 games on the road like Oklahoma State, Nebraska, Kansas, and that sort of thing.

"Being able to plan ahead on bowl trips—which we did this year—is very helpful, but it doesn't always happen. We've learned to make adjustments, especially since the advent of the BCS, and we've learned some things over the years, plus we work with an excellent tourist supplier that does bowl trips and other kinds of athletic travel. We managed to take about 800 people to the Fiesta Bowl when we played Penn State and we had a large crowd that went to the Sugar Bowl a few years ago."

As an arm of the Texas Exes, the Flying Longhorns are an independent alumni group but, Cotton says, "the university is, of course, our great and good friend. In fact, our motto is to praise, promote, and protect the university."

Negative thoughts, therefore, are dismissed with a shrug.

She says the Flying Longhorns "had a great time at Ohio State, because we won the game and they really enjoyed staying at the Blackstone Hotel on campus," although she admits that "a number of people experienced some rather unpleasant things," when they came in contact with Buckeye fans.

"But, we plan to retaliate when they come to Austin this year," she says, grinning. "We hope to kill them with kindness … let them see the gentility of the South."

She also remembers a trip to Louisville years ago that was pretty much a bummer, except for one amazingly upbeat development. "It poured down rain the whole time, and Texas got beaten terribly in the game," she says. "But the Silver Spurs had taken Bevo up there, and it was amazing the way those people reacted. That's horse country up there. They don't see many longhorns.

"It was incredible. They were all just so excited to see Bevo. We even brought him to our tailgate before the game, and a large crowd of people gathered, and they were all standing in line to get their picture taken with Bevo.

"Those charter flights are always fun, especially if it's something like a trip to the Rose Bowl. You've got a whole plane where everyone is dressed in orange, singing 'Texas Fight' across the aisles and then finally singing 'The Eyes of Texas.' Everyone just pretty much has a great time."

The signature trips of the Flying Longhorns are usually a bit lengthier, and do not usually involve hostile fans. In fact, since Longhorns are literally scattered across the globe, and the Texas Exes database currently numbers them at 319,000, you can almost always count on someone flashing a Hook 'em sign at every port of call.

Although Cotten obviously does not go on each trip, she's taken enough of them that she's lost count. "Mike and I have gone on several of them together," she says, "and we've always had a great time. I've been to a lot of exciting places, but one of the greatest things about this job is that nearly everywhere we go, you find Longhorns waiting to meet and greet you.

"It's a great thing, because most people really have a wonderful place in their heart for the University of Texas. Those are magical years when you're in college, and there are so many times when people make real connections again.

"We were on a trip to Greece several years ago, and the first night at dinner we're all sitting around at the table, and these two couples—the wives had been sorority sisters, but neither knew the other was on the trip because the reservations are all made in people's married names. They were stunned and thrilled to run into each other again on the trip.

"On another trip, there were these two couples who each had a granddaughter who was a current UT cheerleader. The two cheerleaders were great friends, but the grandparents had never met each other until that trip. By the time it was over, they were also great friends."

As for Cotten's feelings about the best trips she has ever made, it usually has to do with more than the scenery. "For me," she says, "there are always little vignettes on a trip that make it very special.

"Wherever we go, we always try to connect with local alumni when we can. Several years ago, we were in China—we have a very large Chinese international population on campus—and we went to dinner in Shanghai. We had about 35 people in the group ... and about 25 local alums came to dinner. It was so much fun to be involved with them and see what they were doing.

"They were all very young—most of them MBA grads—and they were all starting tech companies or magazines or something like that, because Shanghai is a very go-go place right now. It's erupting with the beginnings of capitalism in that country, and these people are all involved. For us, it was really a fun experience.

"Another time, I was in Jordan, and we had written some letters to some local people ahead of time, and this one local alum said, 'We want to have the group to dinner.'

"So 18 people on this trip went to this one alum's house for dinner. He had been a student at UT back in the fifties, and he said, 'I remember walking across that campus, and looking up and seeing the inscription, 'Ye shall know the truth, and the truth shall set you free,' and how important that was to him at that time; what an impression it made, and how it affected his life.

"He had gone on to a career where he had been the Jordanian ambassador to several countries around the world. It was just a really outstanding evening.

"All sorts of things happen on these trips because of UT connections. We had a group in Switzerland last summer and they all had lunch at the American Embassy because the ambassador (Pamela Willeford) is a UT grad."

On overseas trips, Cotten says, the average size of the group is about 30.

"We have some larger than that and some smaller," she says, "but we don't like to carry more than 45—that's the number of people who can fit into one motor coach. People like to be together. We also do a large number of river cruises—they're a lot of fun and very popular."

One of the most popular destinations is Italy, but the country presents a slight problem.

"When we have groups going there," she says, "we always have to warn them against putting their horns up. We tell them not to do that under any circumstances."

The Longhorns' beloved Hook 'em sign, it seems, is regarded in Italy as an obscene gesture.

In recent years, the Flying Longhorns have also been affected by world events and natural disasters. But, Cotten says, it's a dedicated and resilient group that eventually forges on, no matter what.

"When Hurricane Rita hit," she says, "we had one tour group down there going to Egypt and another on an Elbe River cruise, and they couldn't get out of Houston, so we had to cancel the trips. It was a little hairy.

"And, there's no question that right after 911 the number of people traveling went down a lot. Right after that happened, we had to cancel a trip to Egypt, and we had to cancel a trip to Africa after more than half of the group dropped out.

"But our numbers are back up now. I think people have made the decision that 'the world is different today and I'm not going to sit at home and miss something I want to do just because the situation in the world has changed.' In fact, this past year we booked three different tours to Egypt, so people aren't even afraid to go to the Middle East anymore."

As for Cotten, her remaining list of unexplored territory is shrinking rapidly. "I would like to go to Vietnam," she says, "because they say it's a great place to visit, and of course it's changed totally since the war. I would like to go to India, and to Mexico to see the Monarch butterflies. And, I've never been to Charleston. I'd love to go there.

"To me, probably the best thing about this job is the continuing connection—to be able to be here on campus and to still be a part of the University of Texas and everything that's associated with it.

"When the football team plays a home game, we have an open house here at the Alumni Center, and the place is packed with people wearing orange, and you see so many people you know. It's one of my favorite experiences.

"All in all, if I could sit down and figure out the greatest job in the world, this would be it. I love everything about it."

21

KEN CAPPS

Hosting Bevo's Party

When Ken Capps received the job offer to become vice-president for public affairs at Dallas-Fort Worth International Airport, he figured life was getting better every day.

He had only one immediate concern—which, as usual, involved the Texas Longhorns.

"When I was offered the job, I said I was very interested in it, and that I would contact them the next day," he says. "What I was going to do was call back the next day and accept the job … and tell them that I would like to wait until after the Texas-OU weekend before going to work. Give myself a little break time."

The next day was September 11, 2001.

"That morning," he says, "I got up and took my son to school. Then the first plane hit the World Trade Center tower. Nobody knew what was going on … people were just glued to the TV, trying to get information.

"Then the second plane hit the second tower.

"I called my boss and got the answering machine, so I left a voice mail.

"Then the third plane hit the Pentagon.

"I just went home, put on my suit, and drove to work. As I was rounding the corner out there, they called back and said, 'We would really love for you to come in', and I said, 'I'm right here.'"

For Capps, 45, it is one of the few days he can remember when the Longhorns were never in his thoughts. "It was definitely a day I'll never forget … just absolutely awful," he says. "We were so much in the thick of everything, and it went on all day long. It was my first day on the job at the world's third busiest airport, and I can assure you that it was memorable.

"I think there were around 200 planes that landed here that were supposed to go somewhere else but couldn't. That's in addition to all the scheduled flights that came in. We had to set them down, get all of the people off the plane and out of the airport, and try to make sure everyone was taken care of.

"They were all scared to death, and so were we—you couldn't help it, not knowing what was going on, whether it was over with or not, or if maybe we were next. But I'm glad I was out here that day, because I think we did such a good job communicating with people and letting them know we were trying to help them. It's definitely one of those days in your life you'll never forget."

Like many others, Capps has a specific feeling of remembrance each year. "Every time September 11 rolls around, it has kind of a surreal place in my heart," he says. "And recently, when they were playing all those 911 calls on the radio during Zacarias Moussaoui's trial, it sent cold chills down my spine. Maybe it touches me a little differently because I was involved in it.

"It's still mind-boggling to me that these guys living in a desert could come in and take down four 747s with box cutters and that they were able to pull it off in such a coordinated way.

"It blows my mind how cool, calm, and methodical they were about killing all those people, and themselves. Our whole country is based on staying alive and saving lives, and their attitude is, 'If I die, I'm a martyr.' Unbelievable.

"I still shudder when I recall the stories about the firemen in New York killed by the bodies of people who jumped out of the tower and fell on them. Can you imagine being up there in one of those towers and having to make a decision like that?

"But I'm very proud of the fact that I could be here and hopefully contribute something, because I'll tell you something: that day, people were absolutely scared to death."

One thing Capps says he is not very good at is providing in-depth analysis of the changes in the airline industry since 9/11. "It was my first day on the job," he says. "I've never known the airline business any other way. I guess some would view this job as glamourous, but there wasn't much glamour involved that day. It was very hard, very stressful.

"I think we're safer. We've certainly tightened airport security—as everyone knows—although at DFW we have it running smoothly enough where you don't have to spend long periods standing in line like you do in some other airports.

"They've made it a whole lot harder to get anything on board that you could use to bring down a plane ... and probably the smartest thing they've done is to harden the cockpit doors.

"But it seems there are constant things that pop up to remind you of it, whether it's Moussaoui's trial or ... recently, I picked up the paper and there was a story about an American Airlines flight attendant who had been scheduled to fly on one of those [9/11] flights. But her father got sick, so she traded with someone and didn't fly—and saved her life.

"Then just recently she got caught up in traffic and someone rammed her car and killed her.

"This really is a great job, and I love it. But it's one of those things where, to this day, you still worry about certain things."

Fortunately, there are other influences around that are fully capable occupying Capps' thoughts for long periods of time ... such as his wife, Laura, and son, Austin, and, of course, the Texas Longhorns.

Should you care to ask, Capps will gladly inform you that he has been a Longhorn since birth. "I was born in 1960 at St. David's Hospital," he says, "which basically overlooks the UT campus and Memorial Stadium.

"I grew up in Austin and got a degree from UT in 1982—bachelor of science in journalism, with high honors—and it has served me well throughout my life (he also has a masters, with honors, from

Northwestern). I'm also a past president of the Dallas Chapter of the Texas Exes, and I've been involved all my life."

But there was one particular moment, he recalls, when all of this seeped into his mind and body and turned him into a die-hard Orangeblood for life. "The year that I really became a Longhorn fan," he says, "was 1969. I can remember that year, sitting on my dad's lap, watching two really momentous events on TV.

"One was the landing on the moon. The other was the Texas-Arkansas game.

"I'm not sure what it was about that game—it still has a mesmerizing effect on me today. I watched the Cotton Bowl game against Notre Dame after that, and it was also a big game … but it's just maybe the buildup toward that Arkansas game that made it so special. But to this day, I remember sitting on my dad's lap and thinking, 'Wow!'"

A few weeks later, in the Capps household, the event was actually memorialized.

"On Christmas Eve, 1969," Capps says, "my dad came into my room—I was already in bed—and he gave me a button that said, 'We're No. 1,' and said Santa Claus had just left it for me. I still believed in Santa at that time, and I went to bed that night, clutching that button.

"My dad died in 1971, and that button is still the most precious gift he ever gave me. I have an office at home full of memorabilia, and I've got that button in there, framed, with an engraving that says, 'Texas Longhorns National Champions—December 24, 1969.'"

Now, it seems, there is another life traveling along a similar course.

Capps points out that Austin is now nine—the same age he was when The Great Awakening occurred—and is "really starting to want to be a part of all this."

Austin, in fact, is probably a little ahead of his dad in that respect. In addition to being named after the city, he was baptized in Barton Springs and has been high-fived by Vince Young.

He also has a special pal, name of Bevo.

This is the result of a rather amazing tradition that has developed in Dallas during the Texas-OU weekend: the annual visit of the Longhorns' mascot to the Capps house for a party. "This has been going on now for seven years," Capps says. "It's gotten to the point where I have people calling me in February saying, 'Is Bevo coming this year?' And I'm going, 'Guys, it's seven months from now—we'll let you know.'"

Among other things, this tradition has fostered a special bond between Capps and the Silver Spurs, who handle Bevo; an expectation of a special treat each year on the part of a nine-year-old boy and his friends, and a palpable air of excitement in a certain Dallas neighborhood each year on the Thursday before the game.

It began as part of a routine aspect of "Texas-OU Weekend"—which as anyone following UT or living in Dallas can attest, is a wee bit more than just a simple football game.

It is a particularly busy time for the local Exes chapter, which schedules a full slate of events for several days leading up to the game, including the "Get Teed Off At OU" golf tournament, which is held on Friday.

"That's quite an event in itself," Capps says, proudly. "I helped get it started 12 years ago. and now it's the largest UT golf tournament held anywhere. I was so impressed ... the first year we held it, in 1994 we donated the proceeds of the tournament in the name of Freddie Steinmark. And instead of just endorsing it or sending us a complimentary letter or something, Darrell Royal actually came up here and played in it.

"He's just such a gracious man, and that really helped get the tournament started.

"Later, one of the things I started doing was to make sure we could arrange to have Bevo come to the golf tournament on Friday, which was a pretty natural and obvious thing for us to do.

"One year, when I was the chapter president, the Spurs came by my house with Bevo on Thursday, just sort of as a courtesy call. And that's how it got started.

"We had a party, everybody brought their kids to get their picture taken with Bevo, and everyone had a great time. Then the next year, people started calling me and saying, 'Is Bevo coming again this year?' So I called the Spurs and said, 'Hey guys, could you come back this year?' And they've done it ever since."

It was the beginning of a special relationship between the Spurs and the Capps. "I really admire the Silver Spurs," he says. "They're such great ambassadors for the University of Texas. I've gotten to know a lot of them personally, and they've always been such gentlemen. And they've always been so nice to Austin.

"One year, he drew a picture for them, and they took it and put it in Bevo's trailer. For two years, everywhere Bevo has gone, that picture has gone with him, and that's neat for Austin.

"The really neat thing for us is that the Spurs have been passing this tradition on from one group to the next, year after year, like 'every year on Thursday, you're at the Capps house.'"

The event has steadily grown in size, and massive preparations are made. "We actually work for weeks getting ready for this each year," Capps says. But it's such great fun, and it's really done especially for the kids.

"The Longhorn Singers—the student choir—also come every year, and it's just a great time. People come and eat barbeque, the choir sings, and the kids get to be with Bevo.

"It's fun to see all these people show up bringing their kids and grandkids—some still in strollers—and they're all dressed up in their burnt orange outfits—it's just a great experience for those kids."

Perhaps the most amazing aspect of it all is that Capps has even gotten an Aggie involved. "We always buy hay and set it out for Bevo," Capps says, "so he can eat and people can sit on it. One of my good friends is a guy we call 'Aggie Mike.' He's an Aggie, but he goes out every year and buys the hay from a dealer in Grapevine."

The party has also drawn attention elsewhere: "When we had the party two years ago," Capps says, "some people pulled up in front of the house and said they were listening to KRLD and got directed here by the traffic report.

"The traffic is always bad, of course, and that year the traffic helicopter spotted Bevo's trailer and started tracking it through the congestion. They tracked it down the freeway and finally they're doing this report like, 'Now it's pulling up to a house over in the Inwood/Lover's Lane area …'"

The next report he wants, Capps says, is "something on *SportsCenter* or ESPN.

"Anyway, this has just become a great thing for us. For me, my favorite days of the year are Thursday through Saturday on OU Weekend. It's running neck and neck with Christmas. In fact, by the time you get to Saturday, it's almost like Christmas Day."

Capps is also making progress on other fronts.

"Right now," he says, "I'm in the midst of building a detached garage onto our house that's going to be the second story. That's going to be my Longhorn shrine. I've got a lot of really cool memorabilia—including an autographed ball from the 1969 national championship team. When I get all this finished I'll call it my Texas Tiki Bar."

Also, with a return pilgrimage to the "Granddaddy" of bowls and a national title, Capps feels he has finally made a connection to a magical moment of long ago.

This time, he wasn't sitting on his father's knee. But strangely—with the pregame buildup and the dramatic come-from-behind victory—it almost felt like it. "I wanted to see the Cotton Bowl," he says, "so we did that first and then hopped on a plane to California. We had had hotel reservations out there for nearly a year.

"I believed Vince Young when he stood up after the Michigan game and said, 'We'll be back next year.' So I reserved the rooms at the hotel shortly after that."

When he arrived, Capps discovered that the situation was perfect. "In my heart, I honestly thought that we were going to win this game," he says, "but out there, absolutely nobody gave Texas a chance to win. To me, that was the best thing that could happen. It removed some of the pressure and maybe put some on them.

"I always feel that way. I hate those games where we're considered a 'lock' to win. To me, that is the kiss of death. I was really glad we went out there as the underdog.

"We were out there for three days, and it never changed. Everyone was sure USC would win."

Capps' confidence soared when he went to a Rose Bowl luncheon and witnessed the contrast in the way the two teams were treated. "It was really funny," he says. "There was a USC table there where they had Pete Carroll, Reggie Bush, Matt Leinart, and some others. They had armed guards all around the table, like they were rock stars or something. I was amazed.

"And over at the Texas table, there was no security—you could just walk right up and take pictures or get autographs or anything you wanted, and I thought, 'I know you guys in California think you're cool … but you're not *that* cool.'"

The day of the game, Capps enjoyed a little cool California hospitality, and bided his time.

"We ran into some [USC] people who invited us to tailgate with them," he says. "They were very nice, and we were very nice to them—I would never be ugly to anyone—but they were, of course, sure the Trojans were going to win."

And they nearly did—but at the end, Capps had the opportunity to feel like a prophet of victory. "In the fourth quarter," he says, "when we stopped USC on fourth down, I turned to my wife and the people we were sitting with and said, 'Congratulations … we just won a national championship.'

"I knew they couldn't stop Vince coming down the field. All day long I had not been sure we would ever stop them. But now, I knew we were going to win."

When it was over, Capps felt like all the other Longhorn fans—elated. But also, maybe a little bit different.

"Sitting there in the Rose Bowl after Texas won against USC," he says, "I had the oddest feeling. I have not had that feeling of absolute euphoria and happiness … since I sat on my dad's lap and watched Texas beat Arkansas, so long ago.

"After the game, we sat there for a few minutes, just taking it all in, savoring the moment—and then we headed out and started walking back to the tailgate. Suddenly, Laura is looking up and she says, 'There's Coach Royal!'

"And sure enough, there he was, sitting in the front row of a bus. So we go running up these stairs and we're saying, 'Coach Royal—isn't this great?' And he grins at us and says, 'Yep!'"

For Capps, there is one specific memory that came home with him, in photographic form.

"At the end of the game," he says, "my wife snapped a picture of me right when the clock ran down to zero. The look on my face is one of sheer joy and euphoria, of a kind you don't get to experience very often. I told her that when I die, I want that picture blown up into a poster for my funeral.

"Because heaven must look like that every day."

22

Fajitas

And so, here was Sonny Falcone: up on the highway, cast adrift in the desert, stranded in the night, wearing an orange sweatshirt that read, "Texas Bigger'n Hell!" and hoping for a ride home.

"In about 15 seconds," he recalls, "the cops got there."

Basically, their first question was, "Have you recently become a lunatic, or is it hereditary?"

"This was outside Lordsburg, New Mexico," Falcone says, "and all of a sudden there were cops all over the place—I mean several squad cars. And the one guy comes up to me and says, 'Where are you going?' And I said, 'Aw, just down the road a little ways.'

"And he says, 'No, where are you going?' And I said, 'Well, I'm trying to get to Austin.'

"And his eyes got big, and he says, 'Texas?'

"And I said, 'Yes, sir.'"

The occasion was a slight glitch in the return trip from the 2005 Rose Bowl by three distinguished gents from Austin—Falcone, Scott Wilson, and John Kelso, who was chronicling the round-trip adventure for the *Austin American-Statesman*.

Falcone had just jumped ship—a development that he blames on Wilson and those danged White Russians. "We were coming back from the Michigan game, and we pulled into Lordsburg and got a motel room for the night," Falcone says. "It's late and I'm trying to get some sleep because I'm driving the next day, but Scott is still having a few.

"So he keeps trying to get me to get up and go get him a quart of milk so he can make White Russians. We got in a big argument about it, and it's kind of funny now, but at the time I just got real upset. So I told him I was going the rest of the way on my own.

"By now, it was about one o'clock in the morning, and I had to walk two or three miles to get back up on the interstate. I took off my coat because it was black, and I was standing up there on the interstate in that orange sweatshirt, thumbing a ride, when the cops showed up."

In the event of arrest, Falcone might have tried to strengthen his position by advising the officers that they were addressing the man who invented the fajita. There has always been some dispute about this in Austin, but the issue is probably a little vague in Lordsburg.

The gendarmes, however, were more interested in getting Falcone off the highway before he became an ex-Longhorn. "They checked me out," Falcone says, "and then the guy said, 'This is a real dangerous place, and we can't let you stay out here. You got any money?'

"I said, 'Yeah, I'm not hurting,' and he said, 'Well, we need to get you on a bus.' I said, 'Fine, I can afford that.'

"The place where they actually dropped me off was a truck stop. The bus came by there, but nobody knew anything about rates or schedules. After about two hours, a bus came by, and there was one empty seat. I took it."

In the end, he says, "I got back to Austin about the same time the other guys did. I think they beat me by about an hour."

Falcone and Wilson, who have traveled together for 15 years to the College World Series and dozens of other venues, were soon reunited. "We got together and blew it off," Falcone says. "He had too much to drink and I lost my cool, and we got into a fight over a quart of milk. But I love that old boy—I've known him since he was a student, and we've been through so much together in all those different places. He's the one who got me started traveling to all these games in the first place."

Though virtually a lifelong fan, Falcone, 68, did not graduate from UT. "I never attended UT," he says, "but I've lived most of my life in Austin, so I became a fan of the local team."

There was one minor faux pas early on, when he named his first child—John David Falcone—after a famous Aggie. "That was before I had developed any allegiances in college sports," he says. "The Aggies were doing well at the time, John David Crow was famous, his last name and my last name—falcon in English—were bird names, that's kind of how my thinking went."

Early on, growing up in the Rio Grande Valley, Falcone's only allegiance was to survival. "I was born and raised in Mercedes, in deep south Texas," he says. "My mother was originally from Mission, and my stepfather, who raised me, was from Monterrey, Mexico.

"He worked in the packing sheds and cotton gins. Down there in The Valley, agriculture was the main thing that was happening. As a kid, I picked tomatoes, chopped cotton, worked in the fields. Did a little sacking at the grocery store. As a teenager, I had a job that paid $5 a day—for Saturdays only—peddling milk. There was a guy over in La Feria who had a milk route that included the air base in Harlingen, so we delivered to the commissary there.

"After high school I did go to college for a while at Pan American. I hitchhiked up there every day, and it wasn't a straight shot—you had to get on Highway 83 in Mercedes to Pharr, then get on 281 up to Edinburg. But we always seemed to get a ride.

"I had to drop out after a year and a half to get a job. So, with 50 cents in my pocket, I hitchhiked to Austin because some of my mother's family lived up here. A guy picked me up on the outskirts of San Antonio and dropped me off at Sixth and Congress, and I've been here ever since. That was in December of 1958."

His first job in Austin was with a boat company, sanding fiberglass. "That was worse than picking cotton," he says. "That powder gets in your eyes and burns like hell. After that, I went to work for a meat company, and I spent the rest of my life in the food business."

Falcone's association with the fajita, he says, began after his marriage to Guadalupe 44 years ago.

"I was working for a meat-packing plant when we got married," he says, "but I was also helping out in a family business. My mother-in-law had a very successful little grocery store in East Austin—about a block from the state cemetery—with a meat counter for over-the-counter-type sales.

"At the time, they were having a little problem keeping the meat cutter sober, so I volunteered to take over the department.

"We had a little stove ... a little burner, and all kinds of meat products, whatever we wanted. I was always fooling around trying to cook something, and that's how I started with the fajitas. One day I just threw a piece of meat on the grill and it cooked up real good. What really got me excited was how easy it was and how quick it could be prepared.

"It took a while before I started doing it outside the store, but one day I told my mother-in-law I was going to try to sell a few tacos down at a festival. It was September 1969. Hispanics always celebrate September 16—it's one of our many holidays—and we went down to Kyle and set up a booth. That's where I made my first sale. After that, I started selling the product here and there, at all of the various festivals in the area. It didn't really take off immediately—a lot it was finding people willing to sit down and try it—but by the late seventies it really became an accepted food item. By then, a lot of people were trying to do the same thing I was trying to do."

Since then, there has been no shortage of dispute over who did what, exactly, and when. Falcone says he was first, and others have made the same claim for themselves. Fajita-lovers, of course, don't really care.

Specifically, what Falcone says is, "I invented the fajita idea."

At one point, he says, "I even tried to get the word registered, but I couldn't afford it."

One thing of which he is certain is that "there sure are a whole lot of people who have jumped on the bandwagon and claimed this is an old recipe that has been in their family forever.

"You can walk in a lot of restaurants now, and it even says on the menu that they are the originator of the fajita. But mine was earlier.

"All I can say is, I hadn't ever seen it, I hadn't ever tasted it, I didn't read about it somewhere, I just started cooking it, and there were a lot of people looking over my shoulder—so-called experts.

"Look, I wasn't here when Christopher Columbus got off his damn boat, so I can't prove he wasn't chewing on a fajita while directing the landing party.

"All I can say is that when I started doing this—with the skirt of the beef, not with chicken, shrimp, or whatever else they're doing now—I was the only one out there who had that product."

A one-time high school catcher, Falcone began traveling with Wilson to the College World Series in 1990, and it became an annual pilgrimage, fraught with predictable escapades.

Recently, however, he has been enticed into a new adventure by Johnny Crawford, a UT fan and alum who has turned cross-country traveling into a lifestyle.

A former All-America swimmer at UT (1951) and later a renowned and highly successful attorney, Crawford, 70, now spends his retirement years traveling from coast to coast throughout the U.S. and Canada with Jerry, his wife of 38 years, in his own personal bus. It is, of course, painted orange and decorated with Longhorns.

The traveling party also includes Jake, a Great Dane, and more recently—with the addition of a trailer towed behind—Falcone and his wife, Lupe.

"I still have a home over in Dallas, in Turtle Creek," Crawford says, "and we have a place in Ruidoso and one in Colorado that we use for skiing. But I'd say we spend about 10 months out of the year in the bus. It's a Prevost. I bought it up in Quebec in 1988 for $310,000. A new one today might cost $2 million."

He has driven it more than 530,000 miles. And at 7.5 miles to the gallon (5.0 in the mountains), it is not an adventure in economy. But Crawford has made a fortune, and now he lives the way he chooses. "This is what I enjoy doing," he says, "but my knees are becoming a problem these days, and if I drive for more than two hours straight, they start to ache. So I needed another driver."

Enter Falcone, who was primed and ready to see the world. After a lengthy journey of several weeks, however, he figured maybe he was seeing too much of it. "We got back from this long trip," he says, "and I said, 'Hey Johnny, maybe I didn't make myself clear—I'm married, and not to Scott Wilson.'"

No problem. Crawford bought the trailer, which has sleeping quarters, bathroom facilities and a stove, and now Lupe has joined the merry group.

Now the entourage spends its time rolling down the highway, enjoying the comforts of home while stopping here and there to visit a famous landmark, check out a lively town, soak in the ambience of a desired location. Always, at the end of the road, there is a Longhorn game.

This can get very interesting. Here, in Falcone's recollection, is Crawford's idea of the sensible way to attend the Ohio State Game. "We left Dallas and drove the bus to Philadelphia," he says, "to visit this eccentric friend of Johnny's. This guy owns an old building in a really rough-looking part of town and lives in it. We drove right in and parked the bus inside the building and locked it up. In fact, there was a couple in an RV that also came in.

"We went out the back door, and there's like a loading dock out there, right near some railroad tracks. We walked across the tracks and waited for this subway-type train to come along, and we got in and it took us to New York. About an hour's ride.

"We wound up in Manhattan. We took a boat for a sightseeing trip around the island, had lunch with an old school friend of Johnny's, then visited the Empire State Building. After that, we visited Ground Zero, then went to a Broadway show. After that, we got back on the subway train and went back to Philadelphia. After that, we drove over to Columbus for the football game."

Among other things, Crawford was once helpful in getting James Street's business career launched, and the two are very close. Crawford is in fact the godfather of Huston Street, who was the American League's Rookie of the Year in '05.

"The Athletics were playing a three-game series over in Cleveland," Falcone says, "and Huston got us on the list for tickets. So we drove over and watched the three games in Cleveland on Monday through Wednesday after the football game. Then we went over to Illinois for Willie Nelson's Farm Aid Concert. We had backstage passes, but my wife and I didn't go back there. I've met Willie before.

"Then we drove down to Branson and stayed there for 10 days, waiting for the Longhorns to come up and play Missouri. We went to the game and then drove back to Dallas."

Later, the bus made it to the Rose Bowl, of course. There was a small problem on the way back.

"Coming back," Falcone says, "we got to Blythe, just getting ready to cross over into Arizona, and the trailer broke down. They had to order parts for it, and we wound up staying there from Friday till Tuesday.

"The beauty of it is, there wasn't anyplace we really had to be, anyway. So that's basically what I'm doing now … just hanging around, enjoying the moment."

23

The Dallas Lunch Bunch

When the Dallas Lunch Bunch held its inaugural meeting 10 years ago, Jack Brown missed it, but he was there the following week and has made every one since then—52 times a year without fail.

In fact, since a very early moment in the group's history, he has been organizing its activities.

"The guy that originally started it really did a great job of organizing it and getting it going," he says. "But pretty soon, his wife had twins, and he had a lot of extra things going on in his life. Then after a while, she had triplets, and we haven't seen him since."

But over the years the other members have certainly seen a lot of Brown, who runs a successful business out of his home (Jack Brown Promotions) and still finds time to organize the weekly luncheons, line up periodic guest speakers, and send out weekly online newsletters.

None of this, of course, has been allowed to interfere with what may be considered Brown's true purpose in life—following the Texas Longhorns wherever fate may lead them, a routine that has been in progress since Dwight Eisenhower was in the White House. His son, Jim, a local tax attorney, is a frequent companion in this crusade.

"I would estimate that I've been to 75 percent of all the UT football games since 1960," Brown says. "And the ones I couldn't get to, I watched them on TV or listened to them on the radio. One way or another, I haven't missed a Longhorn game in 45 years."

For Brown, the world comes in two colors: orange and whatever is left after that. This attitude is reflected in his rules for the Lunch Bunch: If you ain't bleeding orange, you're in the wrong building.

"We've got about 35 to 40 regular members—guys that show up every week," he says, "and it can get up to 60 or 70 or even 100 when we have a speaker, and I've got 400 people on my e-mail list. I'll pick up news articles and send them out twice a week during football season and once a week the rest of the year.

"I never put an article in there that's not positive. We never let anyone speak—for very long—that's not positive. In fact, when we have speakers, I tell them up front: 'If you've got something negative to say, ... go somewhere else.'

"I remember one time I was talking to Mack Brown, and he said, 'You're either for the Longhorns or you're not. And if you're a Longhorns fan, why would you say something negative that only hurts the team?'

"I agree with that."

Jack Brown also sees to it that speakers are well spaced throughout the year—about one every six weeks. "I learned about that from running a bar and restaurant years ago," he says. "If your crowd depends on the entertainment—someday if it's not available, you're going to be sitting in an empty room.

"Our hardcore group of regulars is typically a little older than the regular Exes chapter folks, and above all they're the ones I don't want to lose. If some others want to come listen to the speakers, fine. But our regulars—real dedicated football fans—will be here every week. Now, we've all got a bunch of buddies, and we've blended together real well. This allows us to plan trips together, whether it's a tour of the [UT] facilities or the Rose Bowl, to attend games together, [or] help each other with problems.

"It's kind of heartwarming ... Longhorns bonding with Longhorns. What could be better?"

For Brown, this all began half a century ago in the tiny hamlet of Frost, about midway between Waco and the Dallas–Fort Worth area.

"One of my first memories as a little boy," he says, "were the pictures of Bobby Layne and Bud McFadin on the walls of our house.

"We were sharecroppers, and I don't know if those pictures were there to keep the wind out or what, I just remember them being there.

"I actually started paying more attention to the Longhorns about 1957, when Bobby Lackey was the quarterback, but I was still a little young to really be a fan. By 1960, when I was 10, my older brother, Jimmy, started taking me to some games, and that's when it started.

"We also saw a lot of Baylor games, because the Baptists would take us down to Waco, and I remember watching Ronnie Bull and Ronnie Stanley and those guys. But before long, it was definitely a Texas thing. I can remember the two of us sitting on the couch listening to a game where Texas got tied by Rice, and we just couldn't believe it."

Patience was rewarded; the next year, the brothers exulted, as Texas rolled through a national championship season. "God, what a great year," Brown recalls. "We went to the Oklahoma game and the TCU game and a couple more. I remember sitting in the car at a grocery store listening to the Baylor game, and at the end you could hear the crowd going wild, and they didn't actually announce a score for a few minutes, but I knew we had won because I heard Smokey the Cannon go off.

"We finished up going to the Cotton Bowl game and watching the Longhorns beat Navy. I've still got the five-dollar ticket stub."

Sadly, for the brothers, the joy of being Longhorns fans soon took a dark turn. The following year, at age 29, Jimmy died of a heart attack.

"It was a hard blow," Brown says. "What stuck with me was that before that, Jimmy told me that he didn't think he could go through another season like the one in '63 because he didn't think his heart would take it. He said it as a joke, and for real he had a bad heart, but that has always stuck with me."

In high school, Brown did his part on various athletic fields on behalf of the Frost Polar Bears. Actually, most everyone else did, too. "We were a Class B school then—I think they're Class A now," he says. "There were 12 people in my graduating class, so naturally we all played sports. I played football, basketball, baseball, and tennis every year, and Frost is still the other team I'm a big fan of.

"You know … they're still the two most beautiful animals in the world, polar bears and longhorns."

Brown also began slipping off—rolling down Interstate 35 in the family's red 1957 Ford—down to Austin to watch the Longhorns play football. "It was kind of a funny thing between me and my dad," he says. "He never was that interested in going to the games, and for a while I thought I was putting something over on him. But he knew I was doing it. Even after he called me on it though, I kept doing it. He'd always say, 'Now don't you go down to Austin,' and then I'd get in that car and go.

"I thought I had tricked him … we had our own gas pump, and he had the only key to the lock, but I could still get into it and get gas. I'd use the old Indian trick, and erase my tracks and then unhook the speedometer. He still knew what I was doing.

"I'd go down to Austin by myself—sit on my pillow and drive down. I guess I had my license—I don't really remember whether I did or not."

In any case, Brown says, he never had a problem getting into the games. "One thing you have to remember is that back then, you could get into most games, even the ones with two good teams playing," he says. "I also had an ace in the hole: Abe Johnson.

"He was the custodian for the whole university, in charge of everything, and he would sneak me in. He was really one of my mentors, and I loved him to death.

"Also, his brother, Leroy, lived in Frost, and I'd just go by and pick Leroy up and say, 'Let's go to the game,' and we never had a problem getting in.

"It was also a pretty easy thing to go to the Cotton Bowl every year. You could just buy one ticket—or after I was at UT, I could use my student ticket—and go inside and then wrap it in a game program and pass it back through the chain-link fence to someone else, and get as many people in as you needed to. Then, the whole game we would walk around this big area between the first and second decks, where there were concession stands and all, and just follow the action. We were always right on top of it."

Once Brown enrolled at UT, game attendance became simplified. "During the five years I was there [from 1967 to 1972], I think we played 54 games, and I was at 51 of them," he says. "The only three I missed were played in California."

Early on, he also had what for an awestruck kid from Frost may have qualified as a semi-religious experience. "It was incredible," he says. "All my life I loved Darrell Royal. I just thought he was one of the greatest people ever.

"The first time I ever met him, some of us were walking over by the old baseball field, Clark Field, and he was over across the street, and I swear—he stepped right off the sidewalk and walked straight up to me and shook my hand.

"I can only think of one reason why that happened—I must have had the most awed look on my face that he'd ever seen. Being from the Dust Bowl, he probably looked at me and figured we had similar backgrounds.

"I'll never forget that as long as I live. I was on cloud nine."

As for the most memorable game he personally witnessed as a UT student, there is no question: the battle for the national championship between Texas and Arkansas in Fayetteville on December 6, 1969.

"At the time," Brown says, "I was dating this girl who had once lived next door to Elvis Presley, and her dad owned three airplanes. At first, he just said, 'Hell, I'll just send you up there on one of my planes.' But then the weather got so bad we couldn't get up there that way, so he just gave

us a credit card and said, 'Do whatever you have to do.' We were lucky to
get in there, but we made it."

It was worth the effort.

"Phenomenal game ... just unbelievable," he says. "It was sleeting,
the helicopters were landing, President Nixon was there, Lyndon Johnson
was there, Billy Graham was there, ... Colonel Sanders was there.

"That pass—James Street to Randy Peschel—was the greatest highlight of them all. I was about 40 to 50 rows up and about 10 to 15 rows
from LBJ and George [Walker] Bush. The pass was thrown on the oppo-
site side of the field, so at first you couldn't tell what happened to the
ball—whether it was caught or dropped or went out of bounds or what.

"You just saw Texas fans jump up and cheer, ... and then you knew.
The Arkansas fans had been real nice to us all day, but then they weren't
quite as nice after we scored and they lost the lead.

"When the game was over and we had won, ... we sat there and let
the stands empty, let the fans leave, so they wouldn't bother us. Then we
went down to the field, and I dug up one of the bleachers and dragged it
over to the window of the Texas dressing room.

"Standing up on it, I saw President Nixon presenting the trophy—
they actually did about four retakes for all the media cameras—and we
stood there and watched it all. The funny thing was there were Secret
Service guys all around us, but they never bothered us. Never said a word.

"Afterward, we rushed off to that little airport they had there and
caught the last plane out. Funny thing—on the plane I sat next to (ABC
broadcaster) Chris Schenkel, and he was a mess. He had on plaid pants
and a plaid jacket, and he was just a mess."

A great day, but there was one downside.

"I got about 10 extra tickets and took them up there to sell," Brown
says. "And then there wasn't anybody up there to buy a ticket. It was cold,
it was sleeting, and I couldn't sell a single one of them. I had to bring
them home and give them back to the guys who had financed them. They
were not happy."

Although Brown bows to no one in his fanatical devotion to the Longhorns, some might regard his game face as being a little weird. "These days, Jim and I are usually at the games together, and we really have a great bond," he says. "But he's the loud one. I'm usually pretty quiet.

"Look, a game is meant to be fun, and I understand that. But I just really get wrapped up in the game itself and not all the other stuff. Every play, I'm watching the offensive or defensive coordinator, trying to figure out what he's thinking. It's just something on my mind that I try to stay two or three steps ahead. You can't always do that, but I'm always trying to figure what I would do next in that situation.

"As far as penalties are concerned, I know you're not going to get them overturned—hardly ever—so I don't yell about it because there's really not much you can do. I'll go to a tailgate and visit with people before a game, but I'm not going to drink anything but Coke, or maybe water.

"Now, after a game I'll sit down and drink a beer with people, but I'm too nervous before a game. I also have a hard time eating. Inside the stadium, I just have to watch the game. I can't be concerned about all the other stuff that's going on."

And, although he lives smack in the middle of one of the country's biggest professional sports markets, Brown is pretty much content to stick with the Longhorns.

"To tell you the truth, I'm really not a big pro sports fan," he says. "You know, I respect Curt Flood for what he did—and I respect his right to do it—but when he did it, it ruined all professional sports, just plain and simple."

Brown also figures the whole thing is somewhat deficient from his perspective of atmosphere and fan enjoyment. "I used to have to take peo-ple—customers—out to the Cowboys and Rangers games," he says. "[I] even sat down to dinner with George W. a few times. I just didn't like it, especially the suites. I'd rather sit down in the stands with the people.

"I'd be taking people who didn't want to get there until the third inning, so we could miss the traffic, and then they wanted to leave in the seventh inning so we could beat the traffic again. And I'm saying, 'This is a social event, not a baseball game.'

"I'm from a little town where every kid played Little League baseball, and everyone got enthused about it. It was just different."

Regarding traditions, heated rivalries, and special events, Brown prefers a flexible approach:

"I don't have traditions so much as I have superstitions," he says, "like wearing the same shirt when we're winning or not wearing something associated with a loss. Everything I have here in the house—every cup, every T-shirt or sweatshirt or cap or anything else that I bought at a game, it all comes from games we won. Anything I buy to wear at a game where we lost, I throw it away.

"Rivalries? Well, we've always got Texas A&M and Oklahoma, and if we lose to the Aggies, we have to live with it all year because we're so close. Come to think of it, with all of the damn Yankees that have moved in lately, we have to hear about OU, too.

"Truth is the biggest rivalry is with whoever beat us last."

As is the case with all fans, there are cherished memories—the 1963 and 1969 national champions, the great running backs—Ricky Williams, Earl Campbell, Roosevelt Leaks, Steve Worster, Chris Gilbert, and the many times that Darrell Royal just flat outfoxed the enemy.

In Brown's case, there are also some very long memories. "Bill Bradley was always one of my favorites," he says. "I asked Chris Gilbert about him one time, and he said he could walk on water before he got hurt. I was there in the stands the first time he tore up his knee, against Indiana. It was a piling-on penalty—they did it on purpose.

"Bastards. I hate 'em.

"It's always been that way with me—every time something happens that really hurts the Longhorns, whether it's a severe injury to a key player or maybe a particularly humiliating defeat, I tend to take it personally.

"I still have bad memories of that Holiday Bowl game 20 years ago, when we went out to California to play Iowa, and Hayden Fry beat us 55–17 and poured it on. It was horrible.

"I have never been able to like Iowa since then, and I never will. Sometimes we'll be at a game playing a team that carries that kind of memory, and Jim doesn't understand why I've got this attitude about it.

"Most of the time I really don't want to explain that it's because of something that happened 20 or 25 years ago. I guess you'd have to figure that over time, most people would forget about it and move on.

"But I remember."

24

Traveling Cadillac

In the early summer of 2002, there was ample reason for Scott Wilson to feel that the stars were lined up fairly well and life was looking good.

The Texas Longhorns had just won the College World Series for the first time in nearly 20 years, and Wilson—along with many other exuberant UT fans—was heading home from Omaha. Rolling down the highway toward Austin, whistling a tune.

Suddenly, right before his eyes, an unthinkable tragedy unfolded. He watched, horrified, as his most trusted traveling companion and cherished friend suffered what he recalls as a "massive coronary."

Within moments, a grisly scene unfolded on the side of the road that included every foreboding aspect except a priest.

The victim, presumed deceased, was a 1975 Cadillac painted burnt orange, with horns on the hood and an air horn inside that blared "The Eyes of Texas."

For Wilson, a 54-year-old Austin attorney who is pretty much painted burnt orange himself, it was assuredly the equivalent of losing a family member. For a decade, the two of them, with suitable companions, had been a fixture at UT home games and much of the territory of the old Southwest Conference and Big 12, in addition to traversing many of the 50 states in search of triumph and adventure.

The group was unfailingly convivial—dedicated to supporting the Longhorns, while carrying enough iced-down beer (or White Russians) in the trunk to meet the medicinal needs of everyone. Including the car.

Once, in a moment of youthful exuberance, it had circled the bases at Disch-Falk Field. Now, it lay broken on the side of a highway.

"There were three of us who went up to Omaha together," Wilson says. "We took two cars and were trading off coming back so one guy could rest or sleep. The other two guys were up front in the Cadillac, and I was following in a Miata. I'm just driving along, and all of a sudden— *kaboom!*—there's this huge explosion.

"I thought Osama had hit, or something. Then I looked up and the Cadillac has disappeared in this huge cloud of black smoke. Then it re-appears, and they're pulling it off onto the side of the road. I stopped and we got the hood up, and it was looking pretty bad.

"First, all the coolant started leaking out. Then all the oil started draining out. And at that point, I'm figuring we're not getting this thing started again."

The worst of it was that they were stranded in a strange, foreign land. "We were in Oklahoma," Wilson says, "near Tonkawa. About 20 miles south of the Kansas border.

"The good thing was, there was a whole line of cars behind us full of Texas fans coming back from Omaha, and pretty soon, one by one, they started stopping to see how they could help us. Eventually, I think about 8 or 10 cars stopped.

"One of the reserve players and his parents were in one car, so when they stopped, one of the guys I was with got in and got a ride back with them. We loaded the luggage into another car, and then the two of us that were left got in the Miata and drove home."

Prior to that, however, Wilson made arrangements to have the wounded Caddy towed to Ponca City, a few miles away. Then he called his sister in Austin.

"My sister Nancy—we've always called her Sissy—she's a thrower-away type of person," Wilson says. "I'm a saver-of-things type person. I told her what happened and we were talking, and finally she says, 'Scotty, why don't you just give up on that thing and leave it there?'

"And I said, 'Sissy, you know you can't get a Christian burial in Oklahoma.'"

Soon, Wilson managed to have the car towed 500 miles back to Austin, to a friend's auto repair shop. "It normally would have cost me about $1,200," he says, "but a friend of mine did it for $750. I went out and saw it, and later someone asked me, 'Is the Cadillac OK?'

"And I said, 'The horns are still on the hood and the booze is still in the trunk. It's OK.'"

A search then commenced to find a replacement for the 500-cubic-inch engine that had just blown smoke all over northern Oklahoma. "They finally found one—in Gainesville, I think," Wilson says. "So it's back home and running again."

It is, however, in semi-retirement. "Yeah, it doesn't get out much these days," he says. "There are too many things that can go wrong on it, but the last couple of years I've driven it down to Disch-Falk a few times, and it's been cranked recently.

"There's a group that comes up here from Brenham every year, and one of the guys really likes to drive it, so I let him drive to the ball park."

There was a time, however, when the Caddy got out a lot. Wilson bought it in 1992 and, among other things, drove it to Omaha nine times.

"I tell people," he says, laughing, "that the car told me, 'OK, I got you your damn national championship, now let me rest.'"

As a rough estimate, Wilson figures he has driven the car 50,000 to 60,000 miles. "It's been in 24 states," he says. "As far west as Arizona, north to North Dakota, and east to North Carolina. Me and Sonny Falcone—he's traveled with me a lot—one year we left Omaha and decided we wanted to visit North Carolina on the way back, so we took a side trip.

"Another year, after the College World Series, we went up to Mt. Rushmore and then came back through Denver. One time, a bunch of us were driving down this dirt road in Montana, passing a house about every 10 miles and trying to get back to the interstate, and the guy in the front seat with me reaches over and hits that air horn and plays 'The Eyes of Texas.'

"I asked him why he did that, and he said, 'Because there's a kid standing in front of that house back there with his mouth open.'"

When the car overheated once on a trip to College Station, Wilson says, "We raised the hood and poured the ice out of the ice chest on the engine, then finally started pouring beer on it. We still had to hitch a ride."

Ironically, however, Wilson regarded College Station—for baseball games, at least—as a safe destination.

"I wouldn't take it to a football game over there," he says, "because it would be sitting out in the parking lot unprotected, but at baseball games you can keep your eye on it. Besides, we've always gone over there and partied with the Aggies at baseball games. It's a rivalry, but we always had a mixed group in the parking lot and we got along.

"I guess the worst thing is I've had the horns ripped off the hood twice, once at a TCU football game.

"The first time—when they ripped off the original horns, which were the best—it was down on Sixth Street in Austin."

The devotion to his old trusty steed is typical of Wilson's approach toward the things he figures are truly important in life. It is not necessarily a list that those regarding themselves as "normal" would come up with, but that has never been his concern.

In rough order it has included his family—all gone now except his sister; the Texas Longhorns, his friends, and his job. Did we mention the Texas Longhorns?

Wilson still has the pennant his father bought at the first UT game he ever took him to—against SMU in 1958—hanging on a wall in his house in north Austin.

Of course, a fair percentage of the Longhorn memorabilia in the developed world is hanging on a wall somewhere in Wilson's home. There is a lot more of it sitting around in boxes, waiting its turn.

When Wilson rose from his seat after Texas' dramatic victory in the Rose Bowl, his string of consecutive UT football games attended stood at 344.

In that same three-decade span, he has missed a few baseball games, but not many. During that time, Texas has won four national championships in Omaha, and Wilson has been right there every time, "Jumping up out of my seat like I was shot out of a cannon."

During a 28-year career as an Austin attorney, he has held five jobs—but he is perhaps best known for his association with "The Wild Bunch," a charming group of terrorists who began showing up at UT baseball games back when they were still played at Clark Field. A bit long in the tooth now, many of them are still at it.

The Wild Bunch has never had an official leader—it is not the sort of organization that tends to elect officers—but Wilson, running up and down the stadium steps at Disch-Falk, leading the crowd in chants and orchestrating elaborate pranks, has become the most recognized component.

Though often bizarre, his life has been remarkably consistent, following a relatively straight line for a half-century. The son of Maurice and Nancy Wilson, he was born in a hospital on the doorstep of UT, raised in north Austin, went to McCallum High School and then UT for his undergraduate degree ('72), then to Baylor Law School ('75) and back to Austin for good two years later.

"My father was a salesman, and he got us started going to the games," he says. "I had an older brother, Wade, and my sister, Nancy, who we called Sissy. My mother raised us and then became a nurse when she was 57, and she also sold some real estate. My father and my brother died almost exactly two years apart, in 1974 and '76. My mom died in 2003, so now it's just me and my sister, and we still have the family home over there across the freeway."

He recalls, as a UT freshman when the Longhorns won the national championship in '69, driving up to Fayetteville for the famous showdown with Arkansas.

"There were six of us, all freshmen, in a 1963 Dodge," he says. "Everyone's family gave us food, so we're all crammed in this car, with all the food, and we drove up there. We got there about six o'clock at night and just camped out at the stadium ... back before people were really doing that very much.

"The next morning, there was this big long line for tickets—there were maybe 300 for the whole student body, and half of those went to the band. Everyone who got up to the window could get six tickets, and that's what everyone did. I think we were number 31 out of 36 that made it.

"We had seats on the front row, right behind the Texas bench. We saw Nixon land in the helicopter and Randy Peschel catch the pass from James Street—the whole thing. It was misting all day, but it didn't really matter."

For Wilson, a personal trend had been established. Except for his years at Baylor ("where I learned a lot about how everybody else feels about the University of Texas"), he has been making trips like that all his life.

"I love UT, and I love following the Longhorns," he admits. "I've built my whole life around it."

Wilson began his law career with eight years in the Attorney General's office, followed by two years with the Texas Department of Insurance (formerly the State Board of Insurance). He spent 10 years with the Texas Association of School Boards, two years at the State Board of Public Accountancy, and the past six years working for a health benefits pool of cities with the Texas Municipal League.

"When I first started out, I thought I would be in private practice in three or four years," he says. "I also thought I would be out of this house in three or four years and into someplace nicer. Neither of those ever happened. I've lived here for 28 and a half years, and I've tended through the years to stay in government jobs."

There is a popular notion that he has actually quit jobs because they interfered with his activities as a fan, an idea that Wilson says is purely a fabrication.

Sort of.

"Well, there was really only one case like that, and it kind of happened indirectly," he says. "I left the Attorney General's office because I had a supervisor who suggested that I was actually setting cases in court in a way that would allow me to take my vacation when the Longhorns went to the College World Series.

"He was going to prevent me from going, to teach me a lesson—prove a point—that I should not be doing that. I ended up requesting my vacation at the time the team went to Omaha, and I wrapped up a big case and won it right before I left, and I said, 'I'll see you later.'

"I came back after the series, but I left very shortly after that—and the fact that this guy was hassling me about it is definitely what provided the impetus for me to leave. But that's really the only time I've done that.

"There was a situation later where the Texas Association of School Boards eliminated my job—and it happened right during the middle of baseball season, which was nice because I just took off for awhile. But I really have never lost a job because of this."

An issue, Wilson figures, of whose vacation is it, anyway?

"It's true that I use all my vacation time for that," he says. "I haven't had a non-UT sports vacation in 28 years. I went to New York City in 1978 and stayed a week, and that was the last time. I'm dedicated to being a lawyer, but if this is how I use my free time, it's up to me. People ask me about it and they'll say, 'Well, we went to Puerto Vallarta,' or 'We went skiing in Vail,' and I just say I don't want to go to Puerto Vallarta and I don't ski. It just [matters] whatever your priorities are."

In pursuit of his priorities, Wilson has scrambled and saved to buy game tickets, plane tickets, hotel rooms, food, and gas. He has slept on the ground, in his car, in somebody else's car, on the floor of communal hotel rooms, or on couches in the homes of friends.

He has arrived at destinations cold—no ticket—but has never failed to get into a game. He hasn't missed a football game since October 1977, and estimates he has spent "six to eight months" in Omaha over the years with the UT baseball team.

"This hasn't always been easy," he says. "It's pretty stressing financially.

Hotels?—I've stayed at a few Hiltons over the years, but I've stayed in a lot more Motel 6s. I've stayed in sub-Motel 6s. I've stayed in places I don't even know the name of."

Wilson's lifestyle, shall we say, veritably stands in the way of romantic entanglement. "I've had a few girlfriends," he says. "Even gave a girl a ring once, but it didn't last long. I've still got a lot of close female friends, but I've just never found anyone who wanted to do what I do—to have this lifestyle. I'm certainly not surprised. And if you have a family … you're probably going to miss some games.

"I recently read about an Ohio State guy who has been to a couple of hundred Buckeye games in a row and was trying to find tickets for his wife and kids for a game against Miami. And I thought, if he's been to that many games in a row, those kids are probably total juvenile delinquents."

Speaking of which …

Packed into a section of Disch-Falk Field behind the first base (visitor's) dugout, The Wild Bunch has always seemed to have the same effect on UT opponents as a brushback pitch from Roger Clemens.

Amply endowed with wit, mischief, and ice cold beer, they have tormented opponents and delighted Longhorn fans for a generation, and were considered by former coach Cliff Gustafson to be part of the home-field advantage.

"A bunch of people started that back at old Clark Field before I was involved in it," Wilson says. "But some of us have been in it now since the seventies. I got started with the thing about running up and down the stairs and leading the chants in the eighties, I guess. I just kind of felt like we needed some pumping up."

In between frequent trips to the beer coolers in the parking lot, the Wild Bunch frequently managed to pump up Longhorn rallies and leave frustrated opponents spitting mad with their well-placed insults. They were even better after the game, at all-night parking-lot tailgates or parties at Wilson's house that broke up at dawn. "In the old days, players would show up and party with us, but it eventually became just more of an adult thing, which was just as well," Wilson says. "I never had any problem with the neighbors, because I just invited them, too. A lot of times we would have several hundred people there.

"One night, we killed 13 kegs out there in the backyard."

The house itself is something of a living museum, with every square inch covered with memorabilia. There are Longhorn T-shirts and sweat shirts, pennants and slogans, a letter from Darrell Royal about the '69 team. There are endless photos and almost equally numerous news clippings, covering every room like wallpaper.

In one corner stand several formerly pink flamingos that are now orange flamingos. In another corner sits an Oklahoma football player made out of cow pies. One wall is adorned with the skull of a longhorn, with a bullet hole through the forehead. There is the cap room, with over 2,000 caps hanging on the walls.

Wilson's several cars sit in the driveway, because the garage is filled with a few thousand neatly stacked beer cans ("I lost count at 1,400 about 12 years ago" he says). There are also several unpacked boxes of stuff that people have sent him, because the walls are full.

There is an inscription—a takeoff on the "tan, rested, and ready" routine—that reads, "He's Pale, Limp, Tired and Wasted—Scott Wilson, '88." It sits near the "Texas" slot off the scoreboard in Omaha. Nearby is the old right-field foul pole from Clark Field.

A lifetime of memories, but as the years pass, everything changes.

For Wilson, the hard part got harder a few years ago when his mother began to die, slowly, from Alzheimer's.

"She was still living in the family home across the way over there— the one we grew up in," he says. "She lived there till she died, basically. I stayed over there most of the time for three years taking care of her because she had become an invalid. It actually became a luxury when I could come back and stay over here for a night.

"She spent a lot of time flat on her back. Sooner or later, the pneumonia will get you. People who haven't been through it just don't know what it's like.

"The day she died, Sissy and I stood by the bed and sang 'The Eyes of Texas' to her, about 30 minutes before she died.

"She was always a Texas fan. A Baylor grad, but a Texas fan."

… A final act of love, from a family that has had an abundance of it.

"All my life, she supported me in everything I wanted to do," Wilson says. "Once when I was at Baylor, I wanted to come down for a UT football game, but I had no way to make it. She drove up to Waco and picked me up, and we drove back down to the game. After the game, she drove me back to Waco and then she drove back home.

"She drove 400 miles that day just so I could see a football game, because she knew how much it meant to me.

"My dad had always wanted to see Texas win at the College World Series, but he died in the fall the year before they finally did it, in 1975. So, when I got back from Omaha in '75, I called her and said, 'How 'bout them apples?' and she said, 'How 'bout 'em?'

"I did the same thing when we won in '83 and again in '02. When we won in '04, it dawned on me there was no one for me to share that with anymore. So I came home and … sort of cracked up."

In the aftermath, Wilson talks vaguely about "selling this place and moving back in over there … or maybe fixing this place up so I'd have a normal place to live in. I still have fun all the time, and I always liked to say, 'I may have been to 344 games but I'm mainly here for the party.

"Of course, we're all over 50 now, in the group, and we're not as wild as we used to be.

"In old days when we used to have those parties all night," he says, "the big event of the evening—the big moment—came about dawn: the Paper Catch. The idea was to see who could stay up all night, and go out there and catch the Sunday paper when it was thrown up in the yard. We even had a trophy for it.

"The newspaper lady—she's a real big old gal, must weigh 300 pounds, and she really got into it. It got to be kind of ritualistic: she would pull up and get out of the car and look around, and people would be out there jockeying for position, and she'd say, "Hold it! You know the rules—get back behind the sidewalk. I'm not throwing anything until everyone is behind the sidewalk!'

"It was really funny, and it went on for about 10 years. But finally back about '97 sometime, one morning she pulled up and knew something was wrong because nobody was out front. We were all crashed.

"So she got out and walked the paper up the walk and in through the front door, and looked around. I was lying here on the couch and another guy was sitting in the chair by the door there. So, very gently, she just hands him the newspaper and walks out.

"So, I think we're done with that."

But the rest is what Wilson's life is built around.

"OK, it's had a negative effect on my law career—I'm not a senior partner in a big firm somewhere, but I could never really see myself doing that.

"It really means a lot to me to be a part of all this … to be involved with the university and the athletic teams. I enjoy the people around me. I enjoy knowing everybody at Disch-Falk, and I joke about being the mayor of the ballpark.

"I've seen all 50 states and been places a lot of people have never been. I've been able to be friends with some of my heroes. It's a way that I have become visible, and have come to know people I would never have known otherwise. It's been a lot of fun, and something that's become very much a purpose in my life.

"I've had people try to tell me who I could have been if I had lived differently and hadn't done all this stuff … and my response to that is, in that case, I don't think I'd like what I was very much."

"Sometimes I think my destination in life is just Point B."

25

Rose Bowl Championship Memories

It is probably one of the most surest legacies of the 2006 Rose Bowl that there will be endless legions of Texas Longhorns fans who will remember Vince Young until the day they die.

There are also a couple of Longhorn fans from Fort Worth who will never forget Vince's mother, Felicia.

These would be Marvin and Adam Blum, who had a father-son outing that will surely be enshrined in family legend.

Marvin, a Fort Worth attorney, elaborates: "Although my wife and I are both UT grads," he says, "Adam [a graduating senior] is the real Orangeblood in the family. For me, this was more of a dad experience. For him it was a Longhorn thing, and my passion was watching him enjoy it."

For a while, it wasn't a thing at all. Then the Blums went from "left out" to sitting with elite company on the 50-yard line, courtesy of Frank Denius.

"Frank and Adam have become good friends," Marvin says. "They met traveling on charters to road games, and have really bonded. We couldn't get tickets and Adam was so distraught that he was having trouble focusing on his finals. He talked to Frank, and we suddenly had two tickets on the fifty."

They sat with some interesting company.

"When we got to our seats," Blum says, "we noticed that the families of the players were sitting right in front of us. And there was a woman sitting there with a big orange jersey that said 'Felicia Young' on the back. Everybody else just had the player's last name and a number, but she had her own name on there."

Felicia also had a cell phone and a mission.

"This was the most amazing thing I've ever seen," Marvin says. "We noticed that every time Vince was on the field, she was on the cell phone. I couldn't figure it out. Finally Adam leaned over and said, 'She's on some kind of hot line to The Lord—praying, and asking God to get Vince through this play.'

"She did that the whole game. We talked to her about it after the game, and she told us that it's a prayer hotline—a 900 or 800 number or something—and she's dialing it non-stop throughout the game, praying for Vince, to get him through each play.

"She's a woman of very deep faith, and they just believe that's what gets him through the games."

Blum was, shall we say, awed.

"It was just remarkable to witness that," he says. "For all of us, it's just off the charts as to how you feel in that situation, but can you imagine when it's your son down there? Watching her, I don't know how she kept from passing out.

"Afterward, we hung around talking to her and she was very nice to us. We stood around and visited with her and her mom and her two daughters and the other grandmother. When they came to get her to go see Vince, she asked if we wanted to go with her. We were stunned.

"They brought him up on a golf cart, and when he got off, the first ones he hugged were the grandmothers. One of them has a lot of trouble walking, so they put her on the cart with him. By that time, Vince was moving pretty slow himself, because he was so banged up.

"Later, when we left the stadium, we were helping the grandmother up the stairs, one at a time, and she was having a problem. Felicia was upset because there were no wheelchair ramps and she said, 'With all the money this country's got, they should be helping people that can't get around.'

"The whole thing was just such a unique experience. And when I saw Felicia later at the Davey O'Brien Award banquet, she looked up and screamed, 'Oh, I remember you!'"

Not bad, all in all, for a "dad" experience. Not too bad for the orange-blooded kid, either.

"Adam really does bleed orange," Marvin says. "We went to the Michigan game last year, and afterward he told me we'd be back this year. I wasn't so sure, but he has the faith. He went to all 13 games this year and he yells his head off for Texas no matter whose stadium he's in.

"When the game was over this time, he told me, 'This is the happiest day of my life.'

"I'm glad, but I kind of hope he hasn't peaked at 23. I don't know … his mother and I are both UT grads and fans, but he has so much passion for it. I don't know, something about the genetic mix may have taken him to a new geometric level or something.

"He has a great job lined up in New York, and he says his goal is to make a fortune as fast as he can, and then move back to Austin and go to every single UT game, just like Frank Denius."

For the four members of the Silver Spurs who serve as the handlers for Bevo, the 2006 Rose Bowl is a memory that will never fade.

"It was the trip of a lifetime," says David Dunwoody, most certainly echoing the sentiments of his three companions—Garrett Godwin, George Wommack, and Ross Sutherland.

It was 38 hours between Austin and Pasadena in their custom Ford F-350 truck, with the gooseneck trailer and tack room accommodations for their famous passenger. And the experience was worth every minute.

"Everywhere we stopped, it was the same," Dunwoody says. "We'd roll into some little no-name town and stop to get gas or something, and the reaction would begin. You'd see cars go by, and they'd look and do a double-take, and then you'd see them do a U-turn and come back to look.

"A crowd would gather. You'd start off with five people and pretty soon it would be 100, all waiting to have their picture taken with Bevo. They'd come up and ask, 'Is it really him?' and we're going, 'Yeah, who else?' We were the talk of the town, wherever we went."

Then they hit Las Vegas, and the trip got really good.

"It was an awesome time," Dunwoody says. "We put him up at a stable there, but we couldn't lock him in because they have an ordinance there that in case of fire, the animals in the stable must be able to get out. I wasn't completely comfortable with that, but everyone else was ready to go party, and it ended up all right. At the hotel, we got upgraded for free when they found out we were Bevo's handlers."

Then, they found a friendly crap table. "A great night," Dunwoody says. "We won enough money to pay for the whole trip."

A small potential problem arose when they reached Pasadena, but it was helpfully resolved. "We got Bevo put up for the night," Dunwoody says, "but we heard there were some USC kids who planned to sneak in and throw paint on him, or something. But we had made friends with some guys out there who were troopers in some kind of cavalry on hand there. So we paid them to watch Bevo for us, and we had a chance to go out and see the town.

"They pulled their truck up there by him and stood guard all night. A couple of times a car pulled up slowly, and someone would get out and look around, but our guys would turn on their headlights and the car would take off. So Bevo spent a quiet night.

"When we got to the game the next day, it was wild—there was just a mass of people everywhere, yelling and screaming at us. We almost got into a fight with some USC fans, but we managed to push through the crowd in the truck—with me driving and the other three guys sitting on the roof, yelling back at them and raising the Hook 'em Horns sign."

As the game wound down toward its brain-rattling climax, the four lads found themselves at just the right spot at the right time. "They made us put him back in the trailer with about four minutes left, for safety reasons, and we got back just in time. Vince Young scored that touchdown about 15 feet in front of our faces. It was fantastic.

"Afterward, we charged the field with everyone else, hung out with the players and fans. Then we stood there and sang 'The Eyes of Texas.' Chills went through my spine, and I thought, what a great way to finish my career: here at this stadium, taking care of this beautiful mascot, and winning this game."

The trip back to Austin was about six to seven hours shorter than the trip out, Dunwoody figures. "This time, we skipped Vegas," he says.

For Frank Denius, the Rose Bowl was simply, "one of the greatest college football games I've ever seen."

This takes in a little territory, since Denius has missed only a handful of Longhorn games over the last 60 years, but this one, he figures, had all of the classic elements: high stakes, a supremely formidable opponent, and a dramatic, courageous finish.

"The biggest thing about our '05 Longhorns," he says, "is I've never seen a team more focused on its ultimate goal. With six minutes to play we were down, but you just had no feeling that we were beaten. I noticed this weeks earlier, in the locker room at the halftime of the Oklahoma State game. They were down, but they had no doubt they were going to win. They went out for the second half saying, 'We Believe,' and they played the whole season that way.

"That last play against USC ... you could see Vince look up as he rolled out, and you could tell he had decided to run. You could tell he knew exactly what he wanted to do the whole time.

"I can't fault Pete Carroll for his decision to go for it on fourth down late in the game. I know he got criticized, but I think I would have done the same thing. The way LenDale White had been running, it sure looked like he could make that one yard. And you knew you didn't want to give it back to the Texas offense.

"USC had such a wonderful team … 34 wins in a row, two Heisman Trophy winners, two national championships. A great program, but I think … they had just never faced a team with the overall team speed Texas has. I'm not talking about just the backs, but also people like the linemen and linebackers.

"I'm not any kind of an expert on total football, but I go back a long way, and I think there was as much talent out on that field as there's ever been in a college football game."

At the end, Denius says, it reminded him of another famous game, long ago.

"I remember standing on the sideline up in Fayetteville in 1969, and we were down two touchdowns in the fourth quarter and James Street scored, and he came to the sideline and looked at me and said, 'Don't worry, Mr. Denius, we're going to win this one.'

"And I said, 'James, please don't wait any longer.'"

After two straight years of dispatching a large flock of Flying Longhorns to the Rose Bowl, Betty Cotten has become your basic old pro. "Well, they were both great trips," she says, "but it's different when you have a lot of time in advance to prepare.

"Last year, we didn't know until the last minute. This year, we started making plans after we won the OU game. Last year we just had one option—a three-day package for everyone. This year we had two—a four-day option and then a two-day option with two planes on each. The two-day option was done with the people in mind who made the trip last year and maybe didn't want to stay that long this time.

"This year we had people in several hotels; the team hotel at Century Plaza and then two hotels on the beach in Santa Monica, and an upgrade hotel at the Four Seasons. And, of course, we had our Texas Exes Tailgate before the game, which was fantastic. We sold 10,000 tickets, which was the max we could sell, and so there were 10,000 people there at the party.

"I've heard from so many people who said they ran into people at that tailgate they hadn't seen in years. Everybody had a great time.

"We had one kind of extra highlight—our group that went out of Austin on the two-day program was about 300, and they flew on a brand new United 777, and apparently it was the first one that ever flew in here. So a lot of people who worked at the airport just walked out to watch it land.

"But we started selling packages long before we did last year, and it was a lot easier this time."

When the Longhorns got down by 12 points in the fourth quarter, Scott Wilson recalls, he realized that it was time for decisive action. "I did the only thing I could," he says. "Went and bought two more beers."

Apparently, it worked.

Wilson and a friend were, in a sense, also Flying Longhorns, although their travel options were somewhat different. "We flew Southwest into Ontario—about 40 miles from the Rose Bowl—the day before the game," he says. "We spent two nights in a Motel 6, with the game sandwiched in between, and came back the next day.

"I bought the plane ticket before the OU game for $288, which wasn't bad. But the ticket to the game cost $180."

The previous year, Wilson, Sonny Falcone, and John Kelso traveled to the game in Wilson's pickup truck, a trip that Kelso immortalized in the pages of the *Austin American-Statesman* with a series entitled "Three Fat Guys in a Pickup Truck."

In the closing moments of the game, as the Texas Longhorns launched a desperate drive for what proved to be the winning touchdown, the situation up in the stands was pretty normal.

Joyce Gerrick had her hands over her eyes, and her friend, Bob Turpin, was providing a running play-by-play for her benefit. "She didn't actually see it, but when Vince Young scored the touchdown, she went nuts," Turpin says.

Gerrick points out that she certainly had her eyes open in time to see those scoreboard idiots flash "USC National Champions"—just for an instant. "That was definitely weird," she says. "But the game was beyond belief. It was the game of my life. If I never see another game, I'm satisfied.

"I just can't look at the game when Texas is in distress, which is why Bob had to stand next to me and tell me what's going on. But this is one I'll never forget."

Gerrick arranged all or part of the travel for a large contingent of Longhorn fans from Fort Worth. "A lot of people did their own air, but I did some," she says. "Our group stayed in a little-bitty hotel in Beverly Hills that had about 64 rooms, and I think we had 48 of them. We had about 80 people in all.

"The next day we had two buses for the game. We left at one o'clock—I just figured four hours was enough time for 30 miles, but I didn't realize that when you get there, you can't get in. We should have left at noon."

Once inside, the day began to get interesting. "There were a lot of counterfeit tickets floating around," Gerrick says. "There was one guy there from Dallas who was bragging about all these scalpers he knew, and they had gotten him tickets for $750. When he got up to the turnstile, they took his tickets away from him. He had to bribe a security guard with $250 to give him a wristband so he could get into the stadium, but he had a handicap permit, so later on we saw him sitting in the handicapped section.

"We flew home the next day, and the pilot was a Texas Tech grad and wouldn't say anything about our victory. The flight attendant congratulated us, but he never said anything the whole trip.

"When we landed, I had a few words with him, but I've been floating ever since the end of that game, and I'm going to be excited right into September."

For Bill Trigg and his buddies in the group that calls itself the "Rolling Horns," the Rose Bowl was like the ultimate party.

At the time, Trigg was basically residing in three locations—he has a home in Austin, a business in Houston, and his fianceé, Rose, was living in Aledo, just west of Fort Worth. So, he started early—before Christmas. Trigg rolled his big RV into Fort Worth a few days before the holiday and spent it with Rose. Then they took off.

"We left for the Rose Bowl on Monday, the 26th," he says. "We spent one night out near Lubbock, and then spent a couple of days in Albuquerque, visiting friends. From there we dropped down and went to Indio, California, near Palm Springs.

"There we met up with about nine or 10 more motor homes from our group, and we had a New Year's Eve party outside my motor home. We spent all of New Year's Day at an RV resort and country club there.

"It is definitely the fanciest, nicest RV park I've ever been in. We were looking out over a nine-hole golf course at a lake with a big fountain in the middle of it and a waterfall tumbling down. It was like the Taj Mahal.

"On Sunday, the whole bunch of us drove to Pasadena and rolled into the Rose Bowl together. Eventually, there were about 20 Rolling Horns vehicles parked there. Most of us had tickets for the Rose Bowl Parade, but when you woke up at 4 a.m. the next day and heard that rain hitting the roof, you began to give it a little more thought. All of a sudden, $60 Rose Bowl Parade tickets were going real cheap. I've seen flowers before.

"They must have had four inches of rain that morning, so we stayed in the RV and turned one TV on the parade and the other on the Cotton Bowl and watched both and stayed dry.

"The night before the game we all went to the Texas Exes and Longhorn Foundation party, 'Bash 2006' at the Century Plaza Hotel in Hollywood. There were thousands of people there, and it was a lot of fun."

As for the game itself …

"Just being there was a magical moment," Trigg says. "I went the year before—and just being there in that legendary stadium is a trip. But this was for the national championship, and that made it an even greater moment. Watching Vince Young score the winning touchdown—and seeing the stunned looks on the faces of those USC fans—was incredible.

"They weren't rude to us or anything before the game, but they obviously felt we had no chance to win."

It was such a great moment for the Longhorns, in fact, that nobody wanted to leave.

"We stayed in the stadium for probably an hour and 45 minutes after the game," he says. "And when we left, the last of the Texas players were finally walking off the field. The confetti was all over the place, and as we were walking off I noticed a Texas player—I'm pretty sure it was Rod Wright—lying there on the 30-yard line, making snow angels in the confetti.

"After that, we came upon the media tent, where they were bringing players and coaches in on golf carts to be interviewed. So we just stood by the ropes and watched them bring Vince Young, Mack and Sally Brown, Matt Leinart, Reggie Bush, DeLoss Dodds, Pete Carroll, and several others."

Leaving California, Trigg and Rose spent two days in Tucson and then came home. "In all, it was just over 3,000 miles and a great trip," he says. "At 6.5 miles to the gallon in that diesel, it wasn't cheap, but I just said, 'Hey, you know what? This may never happen again in my lifetime, and I'm going to be there.'"

As the battle in the Rose Bowl proceeded, David Squire wisely paced himself.

"I didn't allow myself to get too involved leading into the game," he says. "I tried to stay levelheaded. I didn't get overly excited when something good happened, and I didn't get overly nervous when something bad happened."

So he was prepared to react calmly when things looked a bit tense late in the game.

"My wife [Misty] looked at me with about 10 minutes to go in the fourth quarter, and I could see the tears in her eyes and she said, 'We're not going to win this game,'" he says. "I said, 'Honey, relax. We've got nearly a whole quarter to play.'

"As it rolled down and we got behind by 12, she was very nervous. I said, 'Honey, we got six minutes left, we're down two scores and we've got the ball. Just wait.'

"We went right down the field and scored, and I looked at her and said, 'If we hold 'em on this next series we win.' And by gosh, we held 'em, and I looked at her and said, 'There's no doubt in my mind we're going to win this football game.'

"I think everyone in the stadium thought that, including Pete Carroll. That's why he went for it on fourth down. I thought it was a great call on his part. He knew if we got the ball back it was over.

"The USC fans were sure they were going to win, and they showed it. They were sure at halftime. I was talking to some of them as we were standing in a very long line to find out they didn't have any beer left. There was no doubt in their minds. But we won it, and then we tail-gated till midnight and flew home the next day.

"It's got to be the best game I've ever seen. It had drama, intrigue, everything."

For Jeff Hattendorf and two of his old college pals, the Rose Bowl was one smooth, quick ride. "We got out there the night before the game," he says, "and just stayed in a hotel out there by John Wayne airport. A friend of mine came out to meet us with a truck loaded down with tailgate stuff.

"We got up early the next morning and were out at the Rose Bowl by 10 a.m. We parked on the golf course there and then set up our tailgate. My friend works at a hotel, and we had the complete tailgate setup—the best one in that whole area."

So they hit the Dos Equis, tossed the burgers on the grill, and fired up the "Vince Young 2-0 Rose Bowl Chili."

"That's what my buddy called it," Hattendorf says. "The recipe, by the way, has been written down and saved for future reference.

"We were surrounded by USC fans, but they were really very nice. One of the groups next to us included Reggie Bush's little brother. He and his buddies played video games all morning. We shared beer, we shared stories—they were surprised that so many Texas fans had showed up. I think that may have been due to all the media buildup of how great USC was, and nobody thought it would be a close game."

Inside the stadium, the crew settled into their $175 seats and watched a classic. The game provided thrills, dramatic twists, a frantic finish and—for the Longhorns—triumph.

"The only thing the Rose Bowl lacked," Hattendorf says, "was cups.

"That was strange—they ran out of cups by halftime on our side. They still had plenty of soda and beer, but they couldn't serve it to you unless you had a cup you had saved. There were people walking around like, 'Hey, I'll give you $40 for your cup.' I wish I'd saved one.

"There were also people trying to buy tickets. We never saw any scalpers, but there was apparently a Rose Bowl vendor walking people in on his badge for $300 each. I saw stories later on the Internet where people were complaining that the only tickets they could find were going for $1,200.

"After the game, we tailgated for about two hours with the people we'd met before, sharing beer, burgers, and stories. They were still nice and said they thought it was a great game—except for the last 19 seconds.

"At seven the next morning, we flew home happy."

In the section of the Rose Bowl where Jack Brown and his son Jim were sitting, there was a unanimous opinion. "Right there late in the game," he says, "we all agreed that if we could get the ball back, we would win the game. We weren't at all sure we could stop USC, but we knew that if we could, Vince Young would get it done for us. He's done it so many times before."

The Browns sat among a knowledgeable group. "We had Vince's high school coach sitting with us, and Michael Huff's daddy," Brown says. "And Vince's mother was sitting behind me. I don't know how that happened, but that's the way it was."

Everyone went home happy, but Brown—who remembers the 1969 Arkansas game the way most people remember the birth of their first child—has a confession:

"To me, that one is still No. 1," he says. "But this one was a very strong No. 2—just a fabulous game. And also, I haven't met anyone so far who agrees with me. Everyone else ranks this as the best game ever. I don't know what it is, but that '69 game has just always meant a lot to me.

"Plus, I had a real good date that night."

This time, he says, "after we got back to the hotel, we stayed up until six in the morning watching *SportsCenter*. We just didn't want to let the moment go.

"We tailgated for about two hours after the game, waiting for the traffic to thin out. When we got back, Pasadena was basically shut down. They have some restaurant laws there where they shut down at midnight, and you couldn't find a place to eat, so we watched TV.

"But it was a great trip. We stayed in Burbank—what a great airport to fly into, not cramped or anything. We got to the game about 11 a.m. the next day and parked way out on that golf course. We found about 15 of Jim's friends right in front of the Rose Bowl—I think they paid several hundred dollars for that spot—and tailgated with them awhile.

"As for the game itself, it really was fabulous, and I can't tell you what a pleasure it was to see all those kids win their first national championship. It was a thrill.

"We've been through hell, and we have a lot of fans who are … a really rough bunch. For a school that thinks it has a God-given right to a national championship, 35 years is a long time."

When Texas beat Oklahoma last October, Rick Gump faced a startling realization. "I told myself then," he says, "that if we go all the way and win the national championship and I don't go to the Rose Bowl, I'm going to kill myself."

Fortunately, Gump immediately set about making arrangements to get himself and his wife, Diana, to the Rose Bowl, and he is still with us today to talk about it.

"I found a Marriott timeshare in Newport Beach that didn't cost us that much, so we flew into John Wayne Airport and got there easily. We got some good airline tickets and went through the [Longhorn] Foundation, where Diana is on the advisory board, and got four Rose Bowl tickets. It all just kind of fell into place."

Except that when they landed, Diana's bag didn't land with them.

"Not a good start," she says. "It was the bag that had nearly all of my UT paraphernalia in it. But it eventually showed up."

Some friends showed up, went to the Rose Bowl Parade, and got drenched. Rick and Diana, somewhat wiser, waited until the weather cleared and played golf.

"The day of the game, we got there at 10 a.m.," Rick says. "Probably didn't take an hour to get there. I was kind of amazed they let us park on a municipal golf course—I parked the rent car right in front of a sand trap. We just walked around, tailgated a little, and enjoyed the moment.

"The game itself was fantastic, with a storybook ending. In our section, there was kind of sinking feeling when we were down 12 points in the fourth quarter—but unlike so many games in past years, nobody got up to leave. There was kind of a feeling of 'We've been here before … this thing isn't over.'

"There was a guy—Longhorn fan—sitting next to Diana, about 50, very conservative-looking. He didn't react much the whole game. Never seemed excited. When we scored that first touchdown, we're all high-fiving … and when we scored the second and went ahead, everybody is high-fiving people 10 rows back.

"Then we looked over at that guy … and he was crying. It was quite a moment—the culmination, it seemed, of something that had been building for a long time."

For Diana, the best moment came, "When they played 'We Are the Champions'—I know it was originally intended for USC, but we had a lot of fun singing it."

Afterwards, Rick said, "we went back, ran into some friends, popped a bottle of wine, and watched it again on ESPN.

"The next day, we went down to Laguna Beach and walked around. There were people all around us wearing orange."

On this occasion, Jay Parmelee was a bit of a slow starter.

It did not actually occur to Parmelee that Pasadena might be nice in January until he sat and watched Texas pound Colorado, 70–3, in the Big 12 Title Game.

"I was down in Houston, watching the game with my nephew," he says, "and when it was over he said, 'You know, we'll never forgive ourselves if Texas goes out there and wins the national championship and we're not there.'"

Thus began the scramble: "I started trying to get tickets and put him in charge of transportation," Parmelee says. "I had to call in a few favors, but we got Rose Bowl tickets through the [Longhorn] Foundation.

"He got us a flight on Continental out of Houston to San Diego, and we drove from there up to Pasadena. Getting into a hotel wasn't a problem, because all those USC fans lived there and didn't need hotel rooms.

"The game was fantastic, and we had a great time. I didn't think anything could top last year. I took the whole family out to the Michigan game and we did everything—Disneyland, the beach, you name it. The kids loved it.

"This time it was just me and my nephew. But we had a ball."

Ken Capps and a large group of friends were among the earlier arrivals at the Rose Bowl—setting up in their tailgate spot promptly at 6:30 a.m. on game day. And, of course, they all parked in Gene's front yard.

"He's an old gentleman who has a house down there about half a mile from the Rose Bowl, right there on the main drag going into the stadium," Capps says. "We parked in his yard the previous year when we went to the Michigan game.

"I found him again this year. I called him about a week before the game and said, 'I'm the guy from DFW Airport from last year,' and he said, 'Oh yeah—I remember you.'

"I asked if we could park there again and he said sure, and I asked him how early we could set up. He said, 'I'm in my eighties now, and I need to sleep until at least 6:30, so give me that much time before you get here.'

"So I brought all my friends, and we all got there at 6:30 and parked in his yard. It's a great place, about a five-minute walk to the stadium.

"I couldn't believe it. When we got there, we saw a big parking sign stuck in his yard that said, 'KEN.' When we left, I took it with me and brought it back home.

"It's funny ... those are kind of ritzy homes in that area, and he could probably sell that house for a lot of money. But he's lived there all his life and doesn't want to move. He lets people park there for UCLA home games. So we had a great spot and a great time."

Capps knew for sure that it would be a good day when he saw the trash truck. "We were set up with our tailgate, watching the people go past and talking with some of them," he says, "and then we look up and this big dump truck comes rolling past us. On the side it says, 'City of Pasadena Trash Truck.' And the guys inside were yelling and waving and honking the horn. When they got right in front of us, they rolled down the window and hung out a sign.

"It said, 'GO HORNS.'"

When a gang of Texas Cowboys rode into town, the sheriff was waiting for them.

It was the old story—a routine worthy of Matt Dillon: "Just hand over your gun belts to the deputy, boys. Then you can head on down to the saloon. We aim to keep Pasadena safe and friendly."

The Cowboys were thus disarmed, but at least they weren't surprised.

"It was the same thing as the year before, at the Michigan game," says Curt Wimberly. They wouldn't let us bring Smokey to the game. They say there's a city ordinance prohibiting firearms inside the city limits.

"But we knew about it beforehand, so we didn't haul the cannon all that way out there for nothing. Evidently it's not a California thing—we were able to take Smokey to the Holiday Bowl two years ago, but Pasadena is different.

"So about 15 or 20 of us just flew to Las Vegas, rented a couple of RVs drove to the game, and just tailgated and had a good time.

"We also saw a great game, so that pretty much made up for it."

James Gumbert's impression of the Rose Bowl is something that rolls quickly off the tongue. "I would say it's probably one of the top ten experiences of my life," he says.

This is especially true since Gumbert and his wife, Kelly Mae, rolled into Pasadena without a ticket and wound up with prime seats to one of the greatest games in history.

There is, of course, a story behind that one.

Gumbert, a member of the Rolling Horns and coach of the U.S. Olympic wheelchair rugby team, was at home in Austin having dinner with friends back in November when he got a call from a friend, Randy Popiel.

"Randy is a pilot for American Airlines," Gumbert says. "I picked up the phone and he said, 'I'm in trouble and I need help … there's a young man who is like a son to us, who has had an accident. He was hanging Christmas lights and fell and broke his neck.'"

Gumbert, paralyzed by a similar accident nearly 25 years ago, said, "What can I do?"

Popiel, it developed, needed help getting his friend transported to a hospital in Dallas.

"We know quite a few people," Gumbert says. "I called my brother, who is head nurse at a local hospital, and we ended up getting the young man transported to Dallas for treatment, and things worked out well.

"It's a common thing with this group of friends we have—we all just help each other out."

"Later, when it was assured that Texas would go to the Rose Bowl, we definitely were not going to miss going, but we didn't have tickets.

"I called a friend of mine in Dallas. Actually he's the guy who was with me when I had my accident years ago, and now he runs a company called Metro Tickets. He said, 'No sweat, we'll get you covered.'"

So the Gumberts headed west with the rest of the Rolling Horns.

"We went out there and did all the parties and everything," he says, "but it got to be two days before the game and we still didn't have any tickets, so it looked like we maybe were in for a disappointment.

"Then we went to a UT Foundation party—just about everybody wearing orange was there—and they were giving away tickets. They had a registration where everyone coming in could sign up for a raffle.

"So, they have the raffle, and they announce that the winner is Randy Popiel. I couldn't believe it. So we all start cheering for Randy, because he's been through so much lately.

"He picks up the tickets, and then walks over and hands them to me, and says, 'These are for you.'

"I said, 'What?' and he says, 'These are yours.'

"I just fell apart ... we had two tickets and sat right behind the band.

"I really can't put into words what that meant to me."

Celebrate the Heroes of Texas Sports
in These Other NEW and Recent Releases from Sports Publishing!

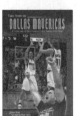
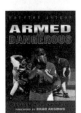
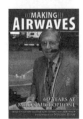